DISCOVER AMERICA'S
FAVORITE ARCHITECTS

DISCOVER AMERICA'S FAVORITE ARCHITECTS

PATRICIA BROWN GLENN

ILLUSTRATED BY
JOE STITES

PRESERVATION PRESS

JOHN WILEY & SONS, INC.

NEW YORK / CHICHESTER / BRISBANE / TORONTO / SINGAPORE / WEINHEIM

This book is for my parents, Virginia L. Brown and Maynard H. Brown, with great love, respect, and gratitude; and for my two children, Eliot and Ginny, with more love than I ever knew was possible.

Copyright © 1996 by Patricia Brown Glenn; illustrations copyright © 1996 Joe Stites

Published by John Wiley & Sons, Inc.

Library of Congress Cataloging in Publication Data:

Glenn, Patricia Brown, 1953 -
    Discover America's Favorite Architects / By Patricia Brown Glenn:
illustrated by Joe Stites.
        p. cm.
    Includes bibliographical references and index.
    ISBN 0-471-14354-5
        1. Architects — United States — Bibliography. I. Title.
    NA736.G58 1996
    720'.92'273—DC20   96-8026

Printed in the United States of America

10 9 8 7 6 5 4 3 2 1

CONTENTS

Acknowledgments vii

What is an Architect? ix

Thomas Jefferson 2

Frederick Law Olmsted 12

Henry Hobson Richardson 22

Louis Henri Sullivan 30

Frank Lloyd Wright 40

Julia Morgan 58

Ludwig Mies van der Rohe 70

Paul R. Williams 80

Philip Johnson 90

Ieoh Ming Pei 98

Selected Bibliography 108

Glossary 111

Credits 115

List of Architects and Buildings 116

Index 117

ACKNOWLEDGMENTS

Discover America's Favorite Architects was a long time coming. A great many people graciously offered their professional help and advice. I want especially to thank Dr. George Ehrlich, Professor Emeritus, Art History, University of Missouri at Kansas City, and Ginny Graves, Director of the Center for Understanding the Built Environment for their valuable advice.

There are too many people to mention by name here, but I want to extend my gratitude to the architectural historians at the State Historic Preservation Offices across the country, private historical societies, and individual homeowners who have given me their time and answered my questions with such patience. A thank you as well to the archivists who made their wonderful historic photographs of all the men and women in this book available to me.

I sincerely appreciate the contemporary architects featured in *Discover America's Favorite Architects* for letting me in your door. The buildings you have designed bring an excitement and immediacy to these pages that may inspire the young architects of tomorrow.

I want to thank my friend, Mike Pronko. He'll never know how his unfailing confidence in me has helped me through this project.

For all the times I was tucked away in my office, trying to meet deadlines or put ideas together, I want to thank my precious family, especially my husband, Christopher, my typist and reader through every page, rewrite, permission check, and cup of coffee brought to my study in the early morning hours.

A thank you to my children: first reader and astute critic, 11-year old Ginny; and typist and commentator, 14-year old Eliot.

To Joe Stites, my illustrator and visionary: your talented hand and funny bone make the people and places in this book come alive. You are wonderful.

And a final thank you to my editors at Preservation Press/John Wiley & Sons, Inc.: Amanda Miller, for her gentle guidance and assurance; and Jan Cigliano, my staunchest ally and the most insightful editor anyone could ever hope for.

If I have failed to mention anyone who has helped me create this book, please excuse the omission; I am most certainly indebted to each and all of you.

Please read, reread, and pass along.

WHAT IS AN ARCHITECT?

Designer... Dreamer... A fulfiller of dreams... Practical... Far-sighted... Planner... Creative... Curious... Environmentalist... Historian.

There is no one way to describe all that is an architect. Perhaps the single trait that they have in common is to meet the needs of their commission while remaining true to themselves. This is not always easy or possible, and often involves compromise on the part of both the designer and the client.

Not all architects are innovators. Some are simply fine designers who use common sense and skill to create a building according to function, dimensions, site, and budget. Others are pioneers who, because of their race, religion, or gender, have braved entry into a field where for so many years they have been unwelcome. Their perseverance and ultimate success have made it possible for others to enter the profession of architecture with self respect.

There are those, who, with tremendous insight have used modern technology and industry to build some of our finest landmarks. They have used new materials and new ideas to formulate innovative styles and in the process changed our perceptions of what architecture is, should be, and can be. Others cannot turn their heads from the past and must rely upon the generations before them to show them the way. Their work is true and honest, good and familiar. There is room for them too.

Fortunately, there are those architects who have cared about our environment: our nation's park land and the beautification of our cities. They have looked ahead—beyond their own lifetimes—to ensure that our inheritance will include mountain ranges, virgin forests, clear waterfalls, rows of tree-lined streets, and city parks in which our children can play. To these designers, we owe a tremendous debt.

Each architect in this book has contributed to the American cityscape or landscape in a unique way. Some have designed residences; others monuments, museums, libraries, railroad stations, churches, parks, entire towns, and more. Each has left his or her signature on the canvas of our country's built environment. Many of our finest architects immigrated from Europe during World War II to escape Hitler, and found sanctuary at our colleges and universities as teachers. Their horrible misfortune has been our immeasurable gain.

This is necessarily an incomplete groups of architects; there are so many who have made contributions and whose greatness deserves recognition. But *Discover America's Favorite Architects* begins here; recognizing these 10 men and women first as individuals and then collectively for their contribution to American architecture. They are arranged in chronological order for easier understanding and to discover how deeply—remarkably in some cases—one has influenced the other or others as the case may be.

In as much as they are different, they share a strong sense of commitment, a powerful and urgent commitment to their ideals through their designs. It is this commitment in the end that distinguishes each architect here and makes our nation so unique, so beautiful, and so great.

A great architect is not made by way of a brain nearly so much as he is made by way of a cultivated, enriched heart. It is the love of the thing he does that really qualifies him in the end. And I believe the quality of love is the quality of great intelligence, great perception, deep feeling.

—Frank Lloyd Wright

Address to Taliesin Fellowship, September 24, 1952

THOMAS JEFFERSON

(1743-1826)

"Architecture is my delight, and putting up and pulling down, one of my favorite amusements."

—Thomas Jefferson

It has been said that if Thomas Jefferson had not also been the primary author of the Declaration of Independence, U.S. Minister to France, President of the United States, and accomplished in so many different areas, he would have gained the reputation he so justly deserved as a great architect. His influence on architectural style in the early nineteenth century was significant, in his native state Virginia where most of his finest works are located, and across the nation.

His keen interest in Roman architecture helped him develop his own style of classicism—sometimes referred to as Jeffersonian but most often as Classical Revival—that presented itself in columns and porticos of churches, banks, schools, government buildings, and even houses. During Jefferson's lifetime, architecture was not thought of as a profession but rather as a

Overview of Monticello, Charlottesville, Virginia, 1768–1809.

hobby that educated gentlemen might pursue. It is all the more remarkable that Jefferson, as an amateur architect, was sought out time and again for designs, opinions, and even urban planning skills. His curiosity was boundless, his thirst for knowledge insatiable and his gifts to our country and our indebtedness to him immeasurable.

Jefferson received an excellent foundation in math and science at the College of William and Mary that was to aid him throughout his career. He became a lawyer and set up shop in a one-room brick house he built for himself on his family's estate. It was here, at Monticello, that he put down roots. The cottage stands today at one end of a U-shaped grouping balanced by an identical building that served as a law office on the other side. Inbetween are stables, servants' quarters, maintenance areas, and at center, the main house. In 1772, Jefferson and his bride, Martha Wayles Skelton, moved into the one room brick "honeymoon cottage" and lived there two years.

It is important to realize that Monticello, from the beginning, was a labor of love and the foundation of Jefferson's life with his wife, Martha. For him, it was a work in process, starting in 1768 and ending in 1809. The house was his passion, and it was here that he initially shows his great admiration of Andrea Palladio, the Venetian sixteenth-century Italian architect whose published works occupied a prominent place in Jefferson's library. In Jefferson's own words, "Palladio is the Bible." By letting Palladio guide him in the language of the ancient monuments, Jefferson was able to adapt classical designs that helped shape our new republic. Working with available local materials and craftsmen, the marble of ancient Rome was transformed into red brick with stuccoed columns and enriched moldings painted white to look like marble. In fact, because there were few men knowledgable in the crafts needed to build Monticello, Jefferson trained them all: bricklayers, carpenters, stonecutters, cabinetmakers, and ironworkers. He was involved in every aspect of Monticello's production. In fact, Jefferson was often consulted by neighbors about their houses; Jefferson designed some, advised on others, and often lent out a workman or two to aid in construction.

In 1923, almost 100 years after Jefferson's death, The Thomas Jefferson Foundation bought and restored Monticello to its former glory.

A trip to France in the late 1780s to serve a term as U.S. minister, and then a prolonged absence from Monticello to carry out government responsibilities kept Jefferson from remodeling the house until 1796. The previous two-story mansion now had three stories and a marvelous portico with colossal columns. The ground floor was enlarged with the addition of a grand central hall, four additional rooms, and piazzas on either side. The crowning glory, however, was the dome seen from the west facade; it was built over the drawing room and borrowed from French and ancient architecture.

Jefferson loved gadgets and inventions and spared nothing to make Monticello more livable. A few examples are: a compass on the porch connected to a weathervane on the roof to tell the direction of the wind; double doors between rooms that opened and closed at the same time; and a dumb waiter in either side of the mantel that allowed an empty wine bottle to be lowered into the cellar on one side while a fresh bottle arose on the other! Stairways and passageways were of great concern to Jefferson, too, and he took pains to keep them as small and inconspicuous as possible. This, in particular, is one of Jefferson's design characteristics that is apparent in other houses he built.

Deeply in debt upon his death, Jefferson's beloved Monticello was sold as a part of the estate. In the end, with hardly a stick of furniture and a few

Monticello was nearly always full of friends and visitors. To make entertainment more pleasurable, Jefferson devised a "dumb waiter table," rectangular in shape, and containing many shelves, which was placed next to each person at the dinner table. All that the guest needed during the meal was immediately at hand thus servants were unnecessary. In this way it was assured that conversation among four people, the ideal number for a meal, was never interrupted.

curtains for privacy, his deep affection for his home was expressed this way: "All my wishes end where I hope my days will end, at Monticello."

Jefferson went to France on a diplomatic assignment between 1784-1789. He lived in a beautiful home with large rooms, some oval in shape, many windows to let in the sun, and elegant classical detailing. He was enchanted with French art and architecture, and surrounded himself with important architects, artists, and thinkers of the day. Among them was the French architect, Charles Louise Clérisseau.

While in Paris, he received a commission to design the new Virginia State Capitol in Richmond. Jefferson felt certain that all three branches of government—executive, legislative, and judicial—should be housed together under one roof. He chose an unusual model for such an assignment: the ancient Maison Carrée at Nîmes. Together with Clérisseau, he prepared plans and submitted a plaster model of the Capitol which they sent across the ocean to America. The plan was simple; it showed a large rectangular space divided into halls and offices with windows cut into the walls for light.

Jefferson introduced the first reproduction of a classical temple for modern use with his Capitol design. Other master builders seized upon the idea, and soon

The Maison Carrée at Nîmes, France, 20 B.C., was the model for the Virginia Sate Capitol in Richmond, Virginia, 1785–1798.

6

the Roman (and later Greek) Revival style was evident everywhere throughout the states.

Jefferson returned from France a far more educated and capable architect. The success of the Richmond temple and news of his work on Monticello made him an authority in the eyes of many. It was for this reason that then U.S. President George Washington and his executive cabinet consulted with him about the new public buildings for Washington, D.C., the nation's capital on the Potomac River. Jefferson was asked to draw up specifications for a design contest for the President's House and the Capitol. James Hoban won the competition for the White House, and Dr. William Thornton was selected for the Capitol building. (Notice the influence of Jefferson in the Capitol dome!) Thornton was replaced by the British architect, Benjamin Henry Latrobe. Latrobe was appointed Surveyor of Public Buildings in 1803 by Jefferson, and remained in that post until 1818.

Pierre-Charles L'Enfant, a city planner from Paris, France, was given the task at this time of laying out the city of Washington. Modeling it after Louis XIV's Versailles, L'Enfant designed a basic plan made up of diagonals and circles. But L'Enfant was too difficult to work with and was dismissed. Thomas Jefferson took on the responsibility for finishing the plans for the new city on the river. He decided on the location of the Mall, the White House, and the Capitol on Jenkin's Hill. Without the organization of Thomas Jefferson at every level of design, Capitol Hill would not have the lovely setting we enjoy today.

Although begun by Frenchman Pierre-Charles L'Enfant, the final design for the city of Washington was completed by Thomas Jefferson.

Marble capitals of columns from a building around the quadrangle at University of Virginia, Charlottesville, Virginia, 1817–1826.

On October 6, 1817, when Jefferson was 74 years old, he laid the cornerstone for the University of Virginia. This was the greatest architectural achievement of his life, and in his opinion, his crowning personal achievement. Often referred to as Jefferson's university, the idea for the state university was his, too. He pushed the legislation through to secure land, designed and supervised its construction, planned the curriculum, hired the first faculty, was a member of the first board, and held the post as the first rector.

Jefferson's vision for the University of Virginia centered around what he called an "academical village," not just a single large building. He described his concept this way: "a small and separate lodge for each professorship, with only a hall below for his class, and two chambers above for himself; joining these lodges by barracks for a certain portion of the students, opening into a covered way to give a dry communication between all the schools, the whole of these arranged around an open square."

Serpentine garden walls at University of Virginia.

The Rotunda on the University campus.

The campus was laid out with buildings to the east and west, bordering a giant green space that lead to a grand Rotunda rising above all on the north end. The south end provided an open view of the mountains and valleys of Virginia. Unusual serpentine brick walls and lovely gardens criss-crossed the backyards of the east and west lawns, while additional dormitory space was provided for students slightly further away on either side of the campus.

It was Jefferson's plan that each building be unique, but more importantly relate to a specific piece of ancient Roman architecture. In a letter to Dr. William Thornton, he wrote that these buildings ". . . shall be models of taste and good architecture, and of a variety of appearance, no two alike,

Poplar Forest, Bedford County, Virginia, 1806. Guests to Monticello literally overwhelmed Jefferson and caused him to seek some peace and quiet at Poplar Forest.

so as to serve as specimens for the architectural lecturer." The orders in these structures, in various combinations include Doric, Ionic, and Corinthian to allow students the opportunity, first hand, to see quality works of architecture. The marble for the capitals was carved in Italy and imported because local stone and stone cutters proved inadequate.

The university's Rotunda was perhaps the crowning achievement of the entire complex, and the influence of its design the most far-reaching. It was a perfect sphere crowned with a dome, and was based on the ancient Roman Pantheon, and measured half its size. Jefferson, however, divided the building into three floors while the real Pantheon was only one large room. There were laboratories in the basement, classrooms and a natural history museum on the second floor, and a library under the dome on top. The Rotunda's design influence was so great that 48 of the 50 state capitols across America are based upon the Pantheon plan.

Jefferson also had a hand in designing many of his friends' and relatives' houses. Perhaps his best effort can be found in his own private retreat, Poplar Forest in Lynchburg, Virginia, designed in 1806. The octagonal design of the house extended to the outbuildings, privies, and even the gardens. Throughout his lifetime, Jefferson retired frequently to this beautiful spot 90 miles from Monticello. Although it was seriously damaged by fire in 1845, it has been faithfully restored and is now open to the public.

So few people on this earth accomplish in one lifetime all that Thomas Jefferson did, and few are so dedicated to their vision. In his 83 years, he helped guide our nation through the Revolutionary War against Great Britain and was a leader in establishing an architectural style that reflected the independence and pride of our new nation.

FREDERICK LAW OLMSTED

(1822–1903)

"What artist so noble . . . as he who, with far-reaching conception of beauty and designing power, sketches the outline, writes the colors, and directs the shadows of a picture so great that Nature shall be employed upon it for generations, before the work he has arranged for her shall realize his intentions."

—Frederick Law Olmsted

Frederick Law Olmsted is recognized by designers and nature lovers as the father of American landscape architecture. Through his brilliant design and administration, he was able to influence the appearance of our country's city and national parks, large city centers and small town communities, college campuses, and private homes. His deep concern about the way America would look tomorrow and great foresight in preserving our natural environment, recreational park space, scenic boulevards, and commonsense urban design all speak to his success as a long-range planner. Olmsted learned his profession through hands-on experiments and experience, and then trained his successors.

Today, across the nation, universities offer graduate degrees in landscape architecture and city planning based upon Olmsted's theories.

Olmsted was born in Hartford, Connecticut, in 1822. He had no real formal education, receiving most of his schooling from clergymen. During his mid-teens, he tried his hand at a number of occupations, including part-time surveyor, Yale University student, bookkeeper, and sailor. He even tried farming on Staten Island, New York. It was there that he learned about plants and machinery for moving earth, and developed his sensitivity toward the shape of the land and its native beauty.

He traveled widely, both at home and abroad, and wrote articles for *The New York Times*. At one point, he received an assignment to visit the pre-Civil War southern states, and his two-volume work, entitled *The Cotton Kingdom*, published in 1861, described life on the plantations. He continued to write and lecture until his retirement.

As a young man, he came into contact with William Cullen Bryant, a writer and poet who belonged to a group known as the New England Transcendentalists, which included Walt Whitman, Ralph Waldo Emerson, and Henry David Thoreau. These men influenced Olmsted deeply, especially in their belief about the absolute beauty of Nature and idea that men and women could find God once they connected with the world around them. This philosophy was to guide him in all of his work throughout his 40-year design career.

There was precious little green space in New York City in the late 1800s. The rapid growth of the city resulted in filth, decay, disease and crime, made worse by loose animals, peddlers, and beggars. Newspaper editorials by philosopher Bryant and the poet Whitman cried out for public parks where

The lovely Bethesda Terrace is a meeting place for visitors to Central Park.

people could get away from all this chaos and find peace and harmony in a little corner of nature.

Olmsted's partner, Englishman Clavert Vaux, 1824–1895.

Andrew Jackson Downing, the foremost landscape designer in America in the first half of the nineteenth century, felt much the same way. He advocated a naturalist English-style park to be located in the center of New York City. But, regrettably, his premature death in 1852 cut short his career and left his British assistant, Calvert Vaux without a partner. Vaux formed an alliance with Olmsted that resulted in the creation of Central Park in New York City, and with it the history of landscape architecture in America truly begins.

In 1853, New York City set aside over 600 acres of land in the center of Manhattan island for a park. A park commission was appointed, and Olmsted was hired as superintendent of park construction. Soon after, a competition for the design of the park was announced and out of 34 entries, Vaux and Olmsted's design was declared the

NEARLY 10 MILLION CARTLOADS OF EARTH AND ROCK WERE MOVED DURING THE CREATION OF CENTRAL PARK.

winner. Greenward, as Central Park was originally called, offered a refuge from the hustle and bustle of New York City. Wholly naturalistic in design, it had several bodies of water, rolling meadows, and wooded retreats. Central Park was carefully planned to look natural despite the fact that it was carefully and artificially organized and entirely man-made. The park design set the standard for parks in cities around the United States, and since its completion, no city has considered itself up to date without at least some recreational green space.

Olmsted and Vaux were geniuses of landscape architecture and together they introduced new ideas to park design. They laid out traffic patterns for bicyclists and scenic pathways for pedestrians to wander, while carriages—and later, cars—traveled along sunken roadways. Streets

APPROXIMATLEY FOUR MILLION TREES, SHRUBS and VINES WERE PLANTED TO GIVE THIS MAN-MADE PARK A NATURAL LOOK.

Central Park evolved between 1858–1880 and is still popular today.

within the park were built below eye level to allow for an uninterrupted view of the rolling hills. Trees and shrubs screened out sights and sounds of urban life, and ponds provided opportunities for skating and boating. Large green squares were designed to be used by baseball, croquet, and badminton players. The promenade (now called the Mall) was the social center of the

park. Thickly shaded with elm trees on either side, the wide avenue led to the Bethesda Terrace, the park's grandest feature. The Terrace was situated on the edge of the lake below the promenade so that a splendid view of the Ramble, or woods, across the water could be seen. Within the first year of its completion, 25,000 visitors enjoyed the park.

"The primary purpose of the park is to provide the best practical means of healthful recreation of inhabitants of the city, of all classes," stated Frederick Law Olmsted. He and Vaux intended to make Central Park a "people's park" from the beginning, and so it has remained for nearly 150 years. More than 16 million people visit the park annually for recreation and reflection, to visit the zoo, attend theater, enjoy a romantic horse and carriage ride, or simply exercise. This is a tribute to Olmsted's farsighted vision of so long ago.

The original design has been altered over the years to make way for the zoo, theaters, and paved streets. Unfortunately, maintenance has always been difficult because the park is so large and problems are expensive to fix. Consequently, during the 1960s and 1970s, the park fell into a serious state of disrepair with overgrown plantings, broken drainage pipes, and vandalism. The city of New York, although responsible for the park, could not pay for its upkeep. Concerned private citizens founded the Central Park Conservancy in 1980 to raise additional money to maintain the park. Now over 50,000 individuals, companies, and foundations in partnership with the New York Parks and Recreation Department have joined forces to save this vital center of New York City life.

Above all else, Olmsted believed in the "healing power of nature." Though he designed many landscapes during his lifetime, he was convinced that there was no substitute for natural, untouched beauty. He was an ardent environmental preservationist, interested in recognizing and saving the national public parks in America. Early in his career he helped draft legislation to help save Yosemite Valley in California, and later he was able to secure the safety of the Sequoia Big Tree Groves throughout the state. Olmsted felt strongly about "the establishment by government of great public grounds for the full enjoyment of the people."

Again with Vaux, he became involved in the conservation of Niagara Falls in 1869. They built sidewalks, planted trees, and designed parks near and around the site. Olmsted awakened public consciousness through his actions and writings about the absolute beauty and necessity to save our scenic landscapes. Thanks to

Niagara Falls, Niagara Falls, New York, 1869–1885.

Olmsted's vision, we enjoy these national parks today, and many more that were established because of the precedent he set.

Olmsted also made a major contribution to community design and development. By the late nineteenth century new towns had grown up outside of city limits, and they were serviced by the railroad. The street plan for these communities usually followed a grid format, but not so Riverside, Illinois, which commissioned Olmsted to develop a town plan. Situated along the Des Plaines River, the site was sloped and irregular. But Olmsted took advantage of the natural topography and allowed roadways—lowered into the ground—to curve and wind in such a fashion as to offer a lovely view of the water. Small recreational parks were scattered throughout the neighborhoods, and a section of the Des Plaines River was dammed to allow for water sports. To ensure a more uniform streetscape, Olmsted suggested that houses be set back from the road a certain number of feet with two living trees between the residence and the road. This idea of a front lawn was certainly an Olmsted innovation.

THE CONVENTIONAL GRID PLAN

THE OLMSTED APPROACH

Despite the fact that population growth has altered Riverside to a certain extent over the years, Olmsted set a standard for community planning to incorporate a comfortable, pretty, and neighborly setting, one that has provided inspiration for other designers in towns across the country.

Riverside, Illinois, 1868–1869.

The grounds of the United States Capitol in Washington, D.C., William Vanderbilt's expansive Biltmore estate in Asheville, North Carolina, and Stanford University in Palo Alto, California (to name but one college campus among many he designed) all speak of Olmsted's importance, imagination, and flexibility as a landscape architect. But perhaps one of his last works, the World's Columbian Exposition in Chicago, in 1893, has had the greatest impact on design—urban design in particular.

Riverside, Illinois. A house set back from the street with a pretty front lawn and shade trees was Olmsted's innovation.

The purpose of the Columbian Exposition was to show off the wonders brought about by the Industrial Revolution and to celebrate the 400th anniversary of the discovery of America. Under the direction of architect Daniel Burnham, architects, artists, landscape designers, and business people worked collectively to create a temporary city on a grand scale that stretched along Lake Michigan on Chicago's South Side.

Olmsted was the site coordinator, and the success of the Exposition was largely due to his brilliant planning and administration. A marshy swampland was transformed into a beautiful city of white buildings. A lagoon became the great central basin for the Exposition's Court of Honor, and vertical terraces were erected where marshes had once been. Great buildings in the Beaux-Arts style rose up to form an entirely man-made environment. Within this master plan, Olmsted focused on pedestrian pathways and scenic views around and between structures. Although not fully realized in the end, the plan shows the railroad station as a central hub for the exhibition. Trolley cars kept people circulating around the site and a moving sidewalk was installed; water transportation was available too.

Olmsted's sensitivity to public spaces and various methods of moving visitors through this urban environment greatly impressed people from all over the globe who came to the Exposition. The idea that architects, city planners, and businesspeople could work together to create such a beautiful place was an exciting notion. Many who came carried their impressions home with them to try out in their own cities. Even in this fantasy environment, Olmsted set a precedent for others to follow in the future.

Olmsted's greatness lies in his sincere commitment to natural beauty and his ability to re-create that beauty through man-made efforts. His great love for the land of America has led to the salvation of thousands of acres of virgin forests, mountains, and waterways. Furthermore, Olmsted's greatness extends to his vision for the future, which unerringly has helped make our nation so magnificent.

HENRY HOBSON RICHARDSON

(1838-1886)

"Let us pause, my son, at the oasis in our desert. Buildings such as this, and there are not many of them, stand as landmarks, as promontories, to the navigator. They show when and where architecture has taken on its outburst of form as a grand passion - amid a host of stage-struck-wobbling mockeries."

—Louis Sullivan on the Marshall Field Wholesale Warehouse, 1885-1887, Chicago, Illinois, H.H. Richardson, architect, Kindergarten Chats papers, February, 1901-1902.

Henry Hobson Richardson became the first American architect to gain international recognition during his brief lifetime—of less than 50 years. His influence was so great that his architectural designs were copied by his peers at home as well as abroad. The style of design that he developed carried his name— Richardsonian Romanesque—and he was the only architect before or since to earn that distinction.

Richardson was a large man and he lived his life in a robust fashion. After completing his education at Harvard University and earning a degree in design from the French École des

Beaux-Arts (he was the second American to attend after Richard Morris Hunt), he returned to the states with a flair for fine clothes and a passion for French conversation.

Richardson's greatest contribution, aside from the development of the Richardsonian Romanesque style, was the promotion of new building types to suit the needs of a rapidly changing country after the Civil War. In the 1870s and 1880s, cities were becoming business centers more so than residential areas—and families moved to the outlying suburbs preferring to commute to work and market by train. These satellite communities required railroad depots, town libraries, public meeting halls, and, of course, houses. In the city, too, Richardson left his mark on the urban residence and the commercial warehouse.

His first major commission, and the one that was to give him an immediate following, was his winning design entry for Trinity Church in Boston, which was built between 1872 and 1877. Here, in this cross-shaped church, the look is massive, geometric, and pyramidal. The transepts, or crossing arms, are steep, and the eastern apse containing the alter is wide; there is a large crossing tower. But what distinguishes the church most is the combination of pink granite block walls trimmed in brown sandstone around the windows and doorways and making up the short columns, or "colonettes." These are all elements of the Richardsonian Romanesque style. Richardson's eye for details and general massing of the church came from Romanesque European architecture dating from around 1050 to 1200 A.D. He did not copy the style of these medieval buildings exactly, but borrowed historic detail to beautify his building designs.

Richardson's first significant work was Trinity Church in Boston, 1872–1877.

This is well illustrated in some of his more mature works, which share this Richardsonian Romanesque flavor, but at the same time find new architectural solutions for building types needed after the war. Nowhere is this better exemplified than in the Marshall Field Wholesale Warehouse in Chicago, constructed between 1885–1887, in Chicago, Illinois. The store was built primarily to service the needs of businessmen traveling to and from the suburbs and the city. It was conveniently located near the railroad tracks and provided a good selection of practical merchandise.

Seven stories high and measuring 500,000 square feet, the Marshall Field Warehouse occupied an entire city block. A building this large is commonplace today, but in the 1880s a typical city street was composed of several small buildings built side by side. Marshall Field, one of the most successful department store owners of the time, thought in terms of an "urban scale" and bought enough land for a single warehouse. This has since become common practice among enterprising businesspeople.

The warehouse had a U-shaped plan and the interior skeleton was made up of fireproof timbers. It is interesting to note that in the late 1800s when new and better building materials such as iron were available, Richardson preferred to use familiar building materials. So the outer walls of the warehouse were constructed of brick and granite with red sandstone trim. Richardson

The stone for the Marshall Field Warehouse was originally reddish in color, but over the years turned a dark, murky brown.

favored a horizontal arrangement in his structures, to give buildings what he described as a "quiet and monumental feeling." To see what he meant, look carefully at the arrangement of granite blocks, the continuous row of arched window heads and underlying sills, the belt course, or thin band encircling the structure, and large decorated cornice or wide decorative molding on the top of the wall above.

The influence of the Marshall Field Wholesale Warehouse was so significant that it set the standard for other large urban buildings of this sort. Sadly, it was demolished in 1930 to make way for a parking lot.

As stated, Richardson had a definite preference for stone and other natural materials. He shared a love of nature and an appreciation for the great American outdoors with major writers, artists, geologists and philosophers of his day. Richardson and his circle saw our country as a beautiful, wonderful paradise, rather than always comparing our heritage to the centuries-old

Ames Gate Lodge, North Easton, Massachusetts, 1880–1881.

treasures of Europe. As a result, Richardson and other architects began to take clues from the forms of nature. One of the greatest leaders of this movement was Frederick Law Olmsted, landscape architect and environmentalist, and a close friend of Richardson. Together they collaborated on many projects over the years, with Olmsted setting the stage for Richardson's creations, and Richardson's architecture providing the perfect profile against Olmsted's magnificent vistas.

One collaboration of these two designers, Ames Gate Lodge in North Easton, Massachusetts, built between 1880 and 1881, is recognized as one of their finest projects. Nestled in a landscape designed by Olmsted, Richardson fashioned a bachelor's quarters with a gardener's potting shed connected to a huge vault stretching over a roadway. Enormous glacial stones piled one on top of the other shaped the wall. The split stone arches of the windows and doorways are original and unusual. The whole complex is covered with a spreading hip roof. One art historian, James F. O'Gorman, referred to this type of Richardsonian architecture as "geological" because it is so dependent upon the earth for its source of inspiration and materials.

Richardson also perfected a new type of structure during the 1880s demanded by urban sprawl and the move to the suburbs: the railroad depot. Hired by the Boston/Albany Railroad to design a string of stations across the

Old Colony Depot, built 1881–1884, in North Easton, Massachusetts, is a particularly fine railroad station by Richardson. It has five arches allowing for easy access, and a broad low roof that extends from the waiting room to the tracks beyond to ensure shelter and shade.

East Coast, he devised a master plan that took into consideration every aspect of the commuter process—most importantly an area for drop-off by carriage and pick-up by trains.

The stations blended into their neighborhoods and acted as gateways to and from the big city. Richardson was careful to use local stone and natural materials so that the entire effect was beautiful and the overall impression one of prosperity.

Small towns along the railroad line were also in need of more community service buildings—first and foremost among them being the library. Richardson stepped in to create a workable, attractive solution as in the Thomas Crane Memorial Library, Quincy, Massachusetts, built 1880–1882. At the heart of this structure is a large reading room, with books in stacks on the upper floors. The library served as a cultural center, art gallery, museum, and

Thomas Crane Memorial Library, Quincy, Massachusetts, 1880–1882.

lecture hall. The building's horizontal emphasis reinforces Richardson's preference for the "quiet and monumental."

Among the many residences Richardson designed, one of the most important was the Mary Fiske Stoughton House, constructed 1882 to 1883, in Cambridge, Massachusetts. The front hall with staircase and fireplace was the center, the heart of this large L-shaped house. The entire structure was covered with wood shingles that formed a skin, or envelope, over the exterior. Once more the horizontal was emphasized by sets of windows cut into the façade. The Shingle Style was not Richardson's creation, although the Stoughton House is among its most beautiful and famous examples.

The legacy of Henry Hobson Richardson is as monumental as his buildings. He was truly an American original who sought to find new architectural forms for an emerging nation after the Civil War. Whether it was a church,

An outstanding example of the Shingle Style can be seen in the M.F. Stoughton House, Cambridge, Massachusetts, 1882–1883.

warehouse, depot, library, or house, he always looked back to the lessons of the École des Beaux-Arts for balance and composition, and toward American nature for its splendor and the awesome inspirations of its natural forms. His friends and associates were the leaders in art and architecture of that time. They included Frederick Law Olmsted, and the younger apprentices Charles McKim and Stanford White (of McKim, Mead, and White, who were to have a burgeoning practice in the late 1890s and early years of the twentieth century). He also collaborated with artist John La Farge and sculptor Augustus Saint-Gaudens, as well as the brilliant contractor O.W. Norcross. Richardson's Harvard University buildings were among the first ever photographed and sold in portfolio format; and even more impressive, his biography, the first written about an American architect, was authored by the knowledgeable and influential Marianna Griswold Van Rensselaer in May, 1988. His was the architecture of the United States, and had he lived past the age of 47 who knows what he might have created. Instead, we must accept Richardson's works of the 1880s as his mature style and look closely at the architecture of Louis Sullivan and Frank Lloyd Wright to see what wonders they wrought from his profound influence.

LOUIS HENRI SULLIVAN

(1856-1924)

"...whether it be the sweeping eagle in his flight or the open apple blossom, the toiling work horse, the blithe swan, the branching oak, the winding stream at its base, the drifting clouds, over all the coursing sun, form ever follows function, and this is the law."

— Louis Sullivan,"The Tall Building Architecturally Considered", 1896

The Great Fire that ravaged Chicago in the fall of 1871 was a major tragedy killing hundreds of people, leaving countless others without homes, and leveling thousands of buildings. Chicago at that time was a busy commercial meatpacking and trading center and the resulting empty acres of ashen land, although a great setback, also provided an unbelievable opportunity for new development. The city fathers, anxious to get Chicago back on its feet as soon as possible and make it an even more beautiful city than it was before, encouraged architects and contractors from all over the United States to come and rebuild the city.

It was about 1890 that a new school of architecture was spearheaded by a small group of talented architects: Burnham and Root, Holabird and Roche, and Adler & Sullivan. The designers of the Chicago School of Architecture, as it came to be known, fashioned the "tall building" with a structural steel skeleton, a greater number of stories and many many more windows. Advances with fireproofing and the introduction of the elevator enabled commercial buildings to soar to unheard of heights during the "skyscraper boom" just before the turn of the century. Sullivan and his contemporaries charged ahead with this new type of construction changing the course of commercial architecture forever.

The "Great Fire" in Chicago was a terrible tragedy but caused the city to rebuild attracting architects from across the Untied States.

Sullivan was born in Boston, Massachusetts in September, 1856. His father was an Irish immigrant and his mother an American. From an early age he took an interest in history and nature and his studies in these fields can be seen later in the exquisite floral designs of his buildings. Sullivan's architectural training, including both formal schooling and apprenticeships with senior masters, amounted to two and a half years. In 1872, at the age of 16, he enrolled in the new school of architecture at the Massachusetts Institute of Technology in Boston. Sullivan soon became restless, finding the emphasis on ancient architecture tedious and boring. By the year's end, he had set out for Philadelphia.

The invention of the elevator made convenient vertical movement within a multi-story building possible.

It was here, under the tutelage of architect Frank Furness, that Sullivan learned about ornamentation and the concept that decorative patterns can beautify a building surface while pulling together all the different architectural elements of a structure.

Sullivan soon moved on again, this time to Chicago where he apprenticed with the leading architect of the day, Major William Le Baron Jenney (formerly an engineer), who was to design the 10-story Home Insurance Building, constructed 1883-1885, which many called the country's first skyscraper.

Within a year, in 1874, Sullivan was once more traveling, this time to Paris to study at the École des Beaux-Arts where other American architects before him (Richard Morris Hunt and Henry Hobson Richardson) had studied. Sullivan stayed at the École for only 18 months and felt about it much as he had about the Massachusetts Institute of Technology. The rigorous program, with emphasis on Old World styles—especially Beaux-Arts—held no interest for him, despite their popularity with many of his contemporaries. The Industrial Revolution that was changing the style of architecture in Philadelphia and Chicago had captured his imagination. He returned to Chicago and realized he was where he belonged.

Together Sullivan and his partner, Dankmar Adler, designed some of the most beautiful early skyscrapers.

In 1875, Sullivan met Dankmar Adler (1844-1900), an established architect 12 years his senior. For a time Sullivan worked as his assistant, and in 1883 the two architects became partners in the firm of Adler & Sullivan. It lasted for 14 years. Adler was the engineer and the businessman of the firm, while Sullivan, with his extraordinary design sense, was the creative genius.

In Chicago after the mid-1880s, architectural design underwent tremendous changes. Jenney's Home Insurance Building of 1885, with its dependence on a steel frame skeleton, was far removed from Henry Hobson Richardson's contemporary Marshall Field Warehouse with its thick, load-bearing walls. This was the era of the tall building, exemplified by Adler & Sullivan in an early and very

The Auditorium Building, 1886–1890, was Adler & Sullivan's first major commission and it was a tremendous success. It did not have steel frame construction, and followed closely the design of Henry Hobson Richardson's Marshall Field Warehouse. Sullivan was a keen admirer of Richardson's having every volume written about him and his work.

beautiful work, the Wainwright Building, in St. Louis, built 1890-1891. Designed with a steel frame skeleton, the block-like building had a U-shaped light court at the center. The tall structure had to follow certain requirements as outlined in 1896 by Sullivan in an article titled "The Tall Building Artistically Considered," published in *Lippincott's Magazine*. It had to have a power plant in the basement, retail shopping on the ground and second floors, office spaces, upper terminals and mechanicals in the attic, and, of course, a common entrance. Each element stated had to be defined in the building's exterior and then woven together to present the building as a total entity. For Sullivan, the form of the building had to mirror its function. He wrote "It must be tall, every inch of it tall . . . It must be every inch a proud and soaring thing, rising in sheer exultation that from bottom to top it is a unit without a single dissenting line."

The Wainwright Building rises from a granite base, the brick piers concealing but suggesting the vertical metal shafts behind them. This vertical emphasis is capped at the top by a heavy cornice thoroughly decorated with baked terra-cotta ornamentation. The spandrels, or panels, beneath the windows are also decorated with baked terra cotta and form a rhythmic horizontal balance to weave the building together into one entire unit.

Wainwright Building, St. Louis, Missouri, 1890–1891.

Although later, in the 1920s and 1930s, the glass boxes of New York would be by comparison real skyscrapers, Sullivan's box-like towers were compelling and different, honestly wrestling with new materials and seeking—although not always completely—to free themselves from the historical styles of the past. Sullivan's greatest strength was his use of ornamental designs. The Chicago buildings of the 1890s all shared the same look and attention to ornament. Their unified appearance strengthened the influence the Chicago School architects and their work had upon each other and architects in other cities.

During the 1880s and 1890s, Adler & Sullivan received numerous commissions for homes and large commercial structures. A young apprentice by the name of Frank Lloyd Wright came to work for them in the midst of their glory days. Wright later referred to Sullivan as "the Master", and perhaps more than any other architect understood and exploited Sullivan's ideas about ornament and function.

The Schlesinger and Meyer Department Store, 1898-1904, in Chicago (later known as Carson, Pirie, Scott) sought to expand its retail space in the 1890s.

This building, perhaps more than any of Sullivan's others, reflected the steel frame of the interior on the exterior. The walls were of glass and white terra cotta, with cast iron ornament framing the ground floor windows and entrance that amazed Chicagoans. The combination of natural and fantastic foliage in that ornament makes Sullivan's work exceptional.

Sullivan was committed to the idea that man must become one with the natural world and felt that through his floral ornamentation people would discover that relationship, and experience a greater joy in their environment.

The Schlesinger and Meyer store's ground-floor show windows, large and rectangular, were framed with ornament and tilted out toward passersby to invite them into the building. The decoration of the doorways and windows provided a sharp contrast to the slick white terra cotta and Chicago-style windows of the upper stories. These windows—large rectangular central panes flanked by double-hung sash windows—created horizontal bands in contrast to the underlying vertical steel frame. A trim of carved ornament surrounded each window, while another band connected the windows.

Sullivan used projecting vertical piers grouped tightly together to form the corner of the building, which stands at a major intersection and extends down the sidewalks in two directions. The building wraps around the corner so as to give a streamline appearance to the whole which looked quite modern at the time of construction.

The year 1893 was an important one for Sullivan. He and Adler had completed the much admired Transportation Building for the World's Columbian Exposition in Chicago. It was also at this time that Sullivan dismissed Wright from his office and terminated his partnership with Adler. Critics disagree about whether Sullivan's architectural career had peaked at this point and whether he continued to design significant buildings on his own. In any case, the number of major commissions given to him diminished (except for the Bryant Building in New York in 1897), and he designed mostly banks in the Midwest during his last 20 years.

Banking in small farming communities began to change around the turn of the century. From 1900-1920, the Midwest experienced an agricultural boom, and the local banks profited by it, and began to see themselves as an important part of the community. This growing sense of economic, social, and political stature of the small town bank escalated to such an extent that

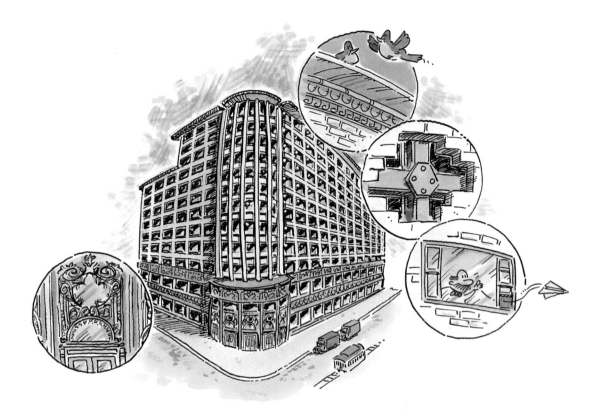

Originally designed as the Schlesinger and Meyer Department Store in Chicago, Illinois, 1898–1904, this building is now known as Carson, Piric, Scott and still maintains a brisk business at 1st and State Street.

they sought to distinguish themselves through their buildings. They also provided community rooms for public meetings, facilities for ladies' banking, and even display cases for local products. Quality service for good clients was their goal, and toward this end, the banks had to become visible in the community.

The National Farmer's Bank in Owatonna, Minnesota, built 1906-1908, is generally considered Sullivan's masterpiece of his later years. The Bennet family, owners of the bank, wanted a modern structure that would stand out from all others by virtue of its design. Sullivan was certain he could deliver just what was ordered, and in a letter dated April 1, 1908 to client Carl Kent

National Farmer's Bank, Owatonna, Minnesota, 1906–1908.

Bennet, he wrote, "I want a color symphony, and I am pretty sure I am going to get it . . . There has never been in my entire career such an opportunity for a color tone poem as your bank interior plainly puts before me."

To be sure, the interior is a kaleidoscope of tone and texture. Each element— walls, moldings, doors, furniture, tellers' windows, light fixtures—is orna- mented with terra cotta, painted stencils, colored plaster, cast iron, and large stained-glass windows. Murals about farming show pride in the town's main occupation. The entire building stands as a "total work of art."

Located originally at an important site where the main business street meets the town square, the building was composed of a large cube connected to a lower two-story structure. Inside, a small hallway leads into a large square lobby. Meeting rooms are near the front, with the vault centered against the back wall. The banking counters form part of an island in the center of the room.

The exterior is beautiful and decorative, but less so than the interior. The façade is divided into three parts with a pink sandstone base and a huge semicircular window at the center framed by brick and terra cotta. The cornice is of the same materials. Cartouches, carved decorative panels of brown terra cotta, fill the upper corners. The building is square and compact, with its sturdy brick façade and heavy cornice, but at the same time open and inviting because of its enormous arched windows and marvelous ornamentation. Sullivan's bank designs were admired and imitated by followers for the next several years.

Louis Sullivan died a lonely and destitute man. Of the more than 150 projects he designed during his lifetime, only 50 remain, and many of these have been restored or altered. It is our good fortune that a portion of the interior of the Chicago Stock Exchange has been rebuilt in the Chicago Art Institute. In addition, many examples of Sullivan's art have been preserved at the Southern Illinois University at Edwardsville.

The great ornamentalist, the promoter of the tall building, and one of the most important founders of the Chicago School, Sullivan was a visionary of the highest order. He followed Henry Hobson Richardson whom he greatly admired and laid the groundwork for Frank Lloyd Wright, who always acknowledged his indebtedness to him.

FRANK LLOYD WRIGHT

(1867-1959)

"Form is to the life as the life is to the form. In other words, the nature of the thing has its own expression according to the materials, according to the method, according to the man. And when the building is of that character, it is beautiful. It has not failed the beauty because it will have the same quality that a tree has, or that flowers have, or that a beautiful human has."

—Frank Lloyd Wright in a letter to G. M. Loeb, January 29, 1951

Frank Lloyd Wright is one of the most well-known, most influential, and best-loved architects in American history. He lived a long life, almost 92 years, and during that time, he grew artistically and philosophically from a talented youth to a brilliant architect and artist. Nature was at the core of all of his creations. As with a blossom or tree, to which he frequently referred, he took into consideration the root, stem, flower and fruit. He called this "organic architecture" and never, in his career, from his earliest rectangular Prairie Style houses to his most sculptural creations, did he stray from this idea.

Historic styles had little place in Wright's work. He felt them to be inappropriate for the time and clientele for whom he built. The modern era required modern materials and methods. Natural materials were used wherever possible but always in the most up-to-date context available. His beloved Taliesin West in Scottsdale, Arizona, is made of the same desert rocks and sands upon which it sits. Fallingwater in Mill Run, Pennsylvania is a part of the cliff and stream from which it emerges. Whether with residential or commercial buildings, Frank Lloyd Wright always tried to place the structure in a harmonious relationship with its surroundings.

Wright believed that people should be comfortable in their environment. Toward that end, especially in the Prairie Style houses, Wright developed an "open floor plan" that permitted freedom of movement throughout the interior and to the terrace outside. Even in the Guggenheim Museum, the sweep of the ramp from floor to ceiling creates an unprecedented way of viewing art and traveling through space in an art gallery.

Wright designed everything in a structure: the furniture, lights, wall and floor coverings, tableware, even clothing for the hostess in some cases! Of the more than 1,000 buildings he designed, he saw 600 of them completed in his 72 years at the drafting board. Wright's influence on American architects through his work, his apprenticeship program at both Taliesins, and his writings are profound and unsurpassed. Modern architecture, as we know it today, is unthinkable without his revolutionary contributions.

Wright was born into a closeknit Welsh family in Wisconsin, in 1867. His father was a lawyer, preacher, and music teacher who instilled in Wright a deep appreciation for music. It is legendary that at every worksite, Wright requested a piano be provided as he was to have said "a symphony is an edifice in sound." His mother was determined that her son become an architect

Wright worked out of his home, built in 1889, and studio, built in 1898, in Oak Park, Illinois.

and brought home from the 1876 Philadelphia Centennial Exposition the Froebel Blocks he played with as a child. Designed by the German educator, Frederick Froebel, the squares, spheres, and cylinders of maple could be arranged in any number of combinations. By age 9, Wright had gained a sense of spatial and structural organization through play. He wrote about this later: "That early kindergarten experience with the straight line; the flat plane; the square; the triangle; the circle! These primary forms and figures were the secret of all effects . . . which were ever got into the architecture of the world . . . All are in my fingers to this day."

His education was uneven; he dropped out of high school, then entered the school of engineering at the University of Wisconsin for two years. Although he did not graduate, he learned a great deal that would be useful to him later. At 19, he left for Chicago, at the time "skyscrapers" of steel frame construction were being built by architects Major William Le Baron Jenney, Burnham and Root, Holabird and Roche, and Adler & Sullivan.

His big break came in 1888 when he was hired by the firm of Adler & Sullivan. Wright quickly became, as Adler put it, "a good pencil in the master's hand," and was allowed to work on their big project, the Auditorium Building.

He married Catherine Tobin in 1889 and built a modest Shingle Style home for his family in the Chicago suburb of Oak Park. Wright's home, like almost every other house designed by him, was centered around the hearth. The low arch brick fireplace, Shingle Style exterior, and steep gabled roof shared a familiarity with Henry Hobson Richardson's designs.

In 1898, Wright moved his studio into his home and built an addition with drafting room, library, and office. Henry Hobson Richardson also had an office at his Brookline residence and Wright, like Richardson, had a full household: wife, six children, and draftsmen. He extended this idea of home/studio later on with his apprenticeship program at Taliesin.

In the 1890s, Adler & Sullivan received many commercial commissions and left the residential work to Wright. It was during these years that he specialized in domestic architecture, building in short order three houses for Oak Park clients. By 1903, Wright had left Adler & Sullivan, and easily won commissions for domestic architecture as well as for two important nonresidential works—the Larkin Building in Buffalo, New York, built 1902-1906, and Trinity Church in Oak Park, Illinois, built 1904-1907.

The important influence of Sullivan on Wright's work cannot be overlooked. Though Wright preferred to work on residential projects and Sullivan on commercial structures, they were both fascinated with ornamentation derived from nature. For Sullivan, it was enough to confine his ornamentation within "the rectangular frame" of his buildings, but Wright saw the organic

Typical floor plan of a Prairie Style House.

possibilities afforded by modern methods and natural materials. He wanted to break free from the "box" and explore the three-dimensional aspects of architecture, which he introduced in the Prairie Style. Although quite different in their approach, Wright forever referred to Sullivan as his "Lieber Meiser" (beloved master) and was indebted to him. Thoughout his life, he experimented with what Sullivan had taught him about structure and style.

The Ladies Home Journal of February 1901 revealed the first plans of Wright's Prairie House. Described as the "city man's country house on the prairie" the plans showed a residence centered around a large fireplace in a cross-shaped layout: the library, dining, and living rooms flowed into one another in a wonderful, open space. The entry and porte cochère, or canopy over the driveway, were parallel to the street. The house was built of natural stone arranged in layers and pinned down by a massive and centrally located chimney. Interior furnishings—rugs, light fixtures, chairs, tables, and stained-glass windows—all were designed by Wright. This plan prompted the building of Prairie Style houses from coast to coast over the next 15 years. In fact, so popular was the Prairie House that a group of architects, modeling their style after Wright, came to be known as the Prairie School. The best among them included Walter Burley Griffen, William Purcell, George Elmslie, and George Mahler.

The Prairie Style was influenced by Japanese architecture. At the World's Columbian Exposition in Chicago in 1893, Wright saw the Ho-o-den Temple with its seemingly transparent walls, simple wood frame, and floating roof. But he insisted that what influenced him most was the Japanese wood block prints with their deep dark outlines, large blank areas of space, and flat ornamental detail. Wright went to Japan in 1905, and again for an extended stay in 1916. He became fascinated with Japanese art and became a collector and dealer.

A "Slat Back Chair" was designed by Wright as a furnishing for the Robie House.

The Prairie Style changed house design forever, and is considered Wright's biggest impact on architectural design.

Wright's furniture was designed with the same clear, crisp lines of his houses. No wood was wasted, and Victorian curlicues were eliminated. Whenever possible, benches and cabinets were built in. Although his chairs were stunning to look at, they were uncomfortable to sit in. Even Wright admitted "All my life my legs have been banged up somewhere by chairs I have designed." Nevertheless, they are regarded among the most stylish of all modern chair designs.

The Frederick C. Robie House of 1909 in Chicago is recognized as Wright's Prairie Style masterwork. Concrete, steel, brick, and glass combine to create a stylish and versatile residence. Built on a long, narrow corner lot, Wright exhibited through his design a complete understanding of open and closed structural space: layers of red brick create parapets or walls around the balcony, while the balconies themselves are shaded by long horizontal

Frederick C. Robie House at the University of Chicago, Chicago, Illinois, 1909.

cantilevered roofs supported by horizontal interior iron beams. Uninterrupted bands of windows let in plenty of daylight and French doors open onto the balcony. The Robie house is exactly what the owner wanted—complete privacy from the outside and total freedom within. The massive central chimney of the fireplace, that holds all the jutting horizontal planes of the exterior in place, forms the central focus for the inside. The family rooms flow one into another without the usual interruption of doors and walls.

The streamlined appearance of the house—continuous windows and exterior decks—recall an ocean liner; in fact, in Germany, where the Prairie Style was especially popular, it was know as the Steamship Style. The airplane, still a relatively new invention, was influential in the Robie design, too: the height of the main roof over the intersection of the crossed arms of the house resemble wings. And, finally, the interior furnishings created for the homeowner resulted in an "entire work of art."

In the then popular *Home and House Magazine*, in a May 1951 article entitled, "One Hundred Years of the American House" the author raved

that: " . . . of these innovators (of the century), none could rival Frank Lloyd Wright. By any standard his Robie House was the house of the 1900s— indeed The House of the Century."

Wright stayed at the Oak Park Workshop, as he called it, for 20 years from 1889 to 1909. At the end of that time his creative energies were drained and his marriage was failing. Anxious to find himself again, he went home to Spring Green, Wisconsin, and began to plan the house that would come to be known as Taliesin. What started as a cottage for his mother became, over several years, a home, a studio, and a farm for Wright, his second wife, family, and apprentices. Situated on the crest of a hill, Wright built Taliesin, Welsh for "shining brow," of cypress wood, plaster from the Wisconsin river, and yellow limestone.

Wright described Taliesin best in his book *An Autobiography* written in 1932, "The whole was low, wide, and snug, a broad shelter seeking fellowship with its surroundings . . . . Taliesin's order was such that when all was clean and in place its countenance beamed, wore a happy smile of well being and welcome for all. It was intensely human, I believe." But tragedy struck in 1914. While working on the Midway Gardens site in Chicago, Wright received a call that Taliesin was in flames. Wright lost not only his beloved home but also his second wife and her two children, together with four other people. All that survived were the studio and farm quarters. Bereft, Wright began to rebuild Taliesin, then left for Japan to work on the Imperial Hotel in 1916.

Sadly, in 1925, a second fire destroyed Taliesin and this time rebuilding it left Wright in debt. His own despair, coupled with the onset of the Depression that gave him few clients, resulted in difficult times. But Wright was too restless to sit quietly. Between 1924 and 1934, he became involved with personal design projects (many were never built), engineering, and large-scale commissions.

By 1932, Wright had married his third wife Olgivanna and founded the Taliesin Fellowship, which changed the way architecture was taught and the way Wright himself practiced architecture. For a small sum, men and women came and lived at Taliesin, immersed themselves in learning about design, and tended to the maintenance of Taliesin's buildings, fields, and livestock. Wright believed that the more the students knew about life from every aspect, the more competent architects they would become. As part of their education they also met and mingled with the most prominent theatrical, political, artistic, intellectual, scientific and philosophical minds of the day. Evenings spent at the theater, watching an international film or listening to a first-rate concert were commonplace.

Many of his contemporaries were critical of Wright's Taliesin program. Once it was in operation, he never hired another draftsman and brought in specialists only as needed. Otherwise, apprentices (all college and university educated) were responsible for all drawing and engineering. Wright openly admitted that the Taliesin apprentices were "the fingers of my right hand." Consequently, some felt students were taken advantage of.

In 1934, Wright turned his attention to a pet project—Broadacre City. He was concerned about the number of people moving away from the center of the city to the suburbs because of the automobile, and he tried to find an alternative that developed suburbia without destroying the importance of the central community. It was not until many years later that Wright's ideas were adopted by urban designers.

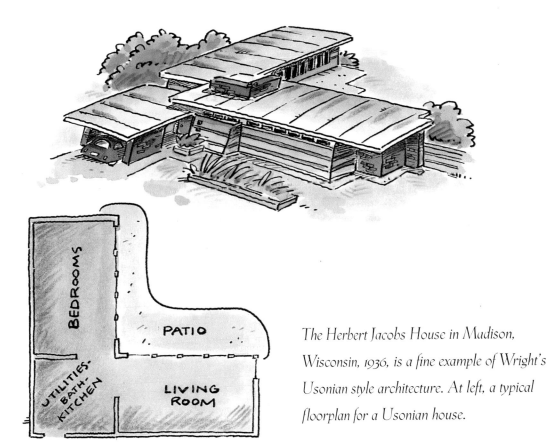

The Herbert Jacobs House in Madison, Wisconsin, 1936, is a fine example of Wright's Usonian style architecture. At left, a typical floorplan for a Usonian house.

Wright also was concerned, after the war, with housing for middle-income families. The so-called Usonian House, another term for American, was one part of Wright's Broadacre plan. Wright showed that houses could be affordable, attractive, and fit into the landscape. One such house, the Herbert Jacobs House, Madison, Wisconsin, was designed and built in 1936 for $5,500: $5,000 for the house and $500 for Wright.

The Usonian house was constructed as simply as possible, having an L-shaped plan with living rooms in one wing and bedrooms in another. The kitchen, utility rooms, bathroom, and dining room were in the center. The core of the house, or "workspace" was tall with clerestory windows, providing natural light. The house was placed off-center on a corner lot

Fallingwater, Mill Run, Pennsylvania, 1936.

and terraces opened off both bedrooms and living rooms towards a garden. The walls were made of inexpensive plywood and covered with vertical layers of board-and-batten siding inside and out. The house rested on a foundation of concrete block, brick, or stone. Plywood bookcases, cabinets, and furniture were built in whenever possible and could be fabricated by the owner.

Each Usonian house was slightly different depending on the needs of the client, but the principles were always the same. To simplify things even further, Wright developed a Standard Detail Sheet to show the design of common parts of the residences. The Usonian house concept was successful and popular from 1937 to 1954, and examples of these homes can be found from coast to coast.

The most dramatic house ever designed by Wright was known as Fallingwater. It was built in Mill Run, Pennsylvania, in 1936 for millionaire Edgar J. Kaufmann, Sr. Using stone, glass, reinforced concrete and steel, Wright created the illusion of a house emerging from a cliff suspended over a waterfall. Built on three levels, the house is a combination of horizontal projecting stone slabs and glass balconies. Each story has its own terrace and stair linking it to the floors below. The concrete and stone piers that support the cantilevered balconies make it possible for them to project over the waterfall. The house is angular and yet merges with the stream below it and trees sheltering it above. The sound of the rushing water is important in the design and adds a soothing dimension. Wright used natural material throughout, linking it even closer to its site. Fallingwater has been described as thoroughly American because of its adventurous and daring spirit of design.

"The conquest of the desert" was how Frank Lloyd Wright characterized Taliesin West in Scottsdale, Arizona, a home and studio he started in 1937 and continued to build until his death in 1959. Situated on 800 acres at the base of the McDowell Mountain range, Wright had to build his own roads to get there. Before construction began, the Wrights and the apprentices camped out in the desert many times to get a feel for the place. "Arizona needs its own architecture. The straight line and broad plane should come here—of all places—to become the dotted line, the textures, broken plane, for in all the vast desert there is not one hard undotted line!"

Taliesin West was not a replica of Taliesin in Wisconsin. It was built of the desert. Rocks of all colors—rust, black, purple, deep yellow, slate gray—were fitted into wooden frames and surrounded by a mixture of sand and cement to hold the stones together. The rough side of the rock faced outward; the smooth faced inward. The pattern was repeated again and again until a wall was formed. The sloping angles of the walls mimicked the rocky cliffs

Apprentices constructed and maintained Taliesin West in Scottsdale,
Arizona designed between 1937–1940.

around Taliesin West. Redwood frames over the white canvas rooftop gave the house the look of a "tent camp," although the canvas was eventually replaced by more permanent material. A kitchen and drafting room/social hall with the Wrights' quarters were at one end of Taliesin West, with the student apprentice quarters behind.

Taliesin West was built almost entirely by apprentices. It was constantly in a state of "becoming," as are, Wright was fond of pointing out, all humans throughout their life. Taliesin and Taliesin West were Wright's most personal works. The magic of the places, as well as the charisma of Wright and his wife Olgivanna's personalities were all part of the experience. But because the Taliesins were built, altered, and maintained by the apprentices, they were owned by them too.

During the final 20 years of his life, Wright designed about half of his total life's work. One of his greatest projects, created at age 69, was the

S.C. Johnson and Son Administration Building constructed 1936–1939 and Research Tower built 1947–1950 in Racine, Wisconsin.

Wanting to provide a better working environment for his employees, Herbert F. Johnson challenged Wright to create something attractive and different on a featureless plain; and so he did. The main 150-foot tower of red brick and glass tubing has soft round corners. What looks like a single story is really two stories tall inside so that the laboratory space has a main square floor and a round mezzanine level directly above it. The floors themselves are cantilevered out from the central core where elevators, utilities and stairs are located.

The exterior of The S. C. Johnson Research Tower, 1947–1950, Racine, Wisconsin.

The most interesting features are the translucent glass tubes that replace the conventional window. They provide a wall surface, texture and light at the same time.

The Research Tower is an example of how Wright used "organic" references whenever possible. Here, the image of a tree trunk forms the "core," and the outstretched "branches" comprise the different floor levels in the tower. The gently rounded corners of the tower, appear pliable or "plastic."

The interior of the Administration Building, 1936–1939, with its unusual lily pad–like columns.

Once inside the Administration Building, we can see that Wright has taken his "organic" idea even farther. Here, tall white columns of concrete sprayed over a mesh frame rise out of the workroom floor and spread like lily pads against the ceiling. Each capable of bearing 60 tons, the columns fan out to support the roof and at the same time let light filter in. The exterior walls have no real supporting function. This forest of columns is found in the main workroom.

Partitions are made of the same glass tubes used in the tower, ceiling, and cornice. Bridges and balconies overlook the main room. The physical environment encouraged comraderie among Johnson Wax employees. Tea time was a ritual, and there was even a company choir. Wright created a feeling of comfort, ease, and goodwill in his buildings, which resulted in higher productivity.

The 1950s were busy times for Wright. The number and variety of buildings he designed—gas stations, synagogues, birdhouses, and the Price Tower in Bartlesville, Oklahoma—kept him fully occupied. Ironically, his last and perhaps best-known masterpiece he would never even see completed. The Solomon R. Guggenheim Museum in New York City, New York, was completed in 1959 just six months after his death. Although it was controversial, it was a magnificent structure—architec-

A final masterpiece and work of art in its own right is the Solomon R. Guggenheim Museum, New York City, 1943–1959.

ture as sculpture. For Wright, the Guggenheim realized the ultimate organic plastic form.

The museum stands across from Central Park at 88th Street and Fifth Avenue and occupies an entire block. Best described as a giant corkscrew, the main building is tucked tightly into the corner. A continuous interior ramp, or walkway, runs from floor to ceiling, narrowing as it ascends. The paintings are hung on the outer walls of the ramp and in the many small semicircular viewing niches. The paintings are tilted away from the walls so as to appear on an easel. Wright believed the best way to view an exhibition here was to take the elevator to the top and meander down. In this way, the exhibition could be seen in chronological order.

Natural light comes from the skylight above, and artificial incandescent lights provide shifting light sources. This museum was designed for modern artists, and in this wonderful concrete and steel swirling design, Wright created a different and nontraditional gallery space. However, the gallery never looked as Wright imagined it. When opened in 1959, the museum director made many changes and it was not until 1991 to 1992, when the building underwent a restoration did it more closely resemble Wright's original design.

Frank Lloyd Wright continued to practice architecture into his late 80s and early 90s. He survived yet another fire at Taliesin at Spring Green in 1952 at age 85 and set about restoration and changes.

During his lifetime Wright also wrote many books and articles, and he lectured widely. After World War II in the mid-1940s he received many awards and honors, to name a few: the English Royal Gold Medal for Architecture, the Medici Medal at Palazzo Vecchio in Florence (the first time given to an American), the Star of Solidarity at the Doges Palace in Venice, and the Gold Medal from the American Institute of Architects. Just prior to his death in 1959, he received an honorary doctorate from the University of Wales at Bangor.

In the Frank Lloyd Wright archives at Taliesin West reside more than 21,000 original plans, sketches and drawings—in color and full detail—of all the different types of architecture he designed. Wright was a critic and collector, as well as a philosopher, and to his list of accomplishments are books he wrote about Japanese art, wood blocks in particular. He was also an environmentalist and urban planner, as witnessed by Broadacre City and the Usonian house. In 1940, The Frank Lloyd Wright Foundation was established to further his creative ideas—many of them yet to be fully realized. Wright described his many achievements best in an address to the Taliesin

Fellowship in 1954: "There is no such thing as an architect who is but one thing, or limited in his views, in his outlook. He must be the most comprehensive of all the masters, most comprehensive of all the human beings on earth. His work is the thing that is entrusted to him by way of his virtue, is most broad of all."

JULIA MORGAN

(1872-1957)

Her office was a real apprenticeship. To work with her was to work from the ground up, and it had certain drawbacks because you learned to be so thorough that you couldn't put your pen down unless it meant something . . . She would say, "Think it out at the start and finish everything as you go along."

–Dorothy Wormser Coblentz employed by Julia Morgan

Even before women won the right to vote for president of the United States architect Julia Morgan had designed nearly 100 buildings in California by 1911. By that date she had accumulated an armload of "firsts" in her career that earned her recognition as an outstanding architect and strong advocate for women's rights. Morgan was the first woman to graduate from the University of California, Berkeley, with a degree in Civil Engineering. In 1901, at the age of 29, she was first to receive her Certificat d'Étude in architecture from the École des Beaux-Arts in Paris, the world-famous school of architecture that had previously admitted only men. In 1904, she was the first woman to receive an architect's license in the state of California.

While at the University of California, she came into contact with the prominent architect Bernard Maybeck. He had arrived in Berkeley in 1894, a year before Morgan graduated. He had studied at the École des Beaux-Arts and worked in New York City, Kansas City, and San Francisco. He was a magnet for students wishing to learn design and the art of architecture as engineering was not concerned with those issues. Morgan eagerly attended informal classes held in Maybeck's home and later worked with him on the Phoebe Apperson Hearst Gymnasium at the University of California, Berkeley. Maybeck was instrumental in encouraging Morgan to attend the École. She carried with her all her life his ideas about the power of good design to communicate feeling, and believed as he did that: "With four sticks of wood you can express any human emotion."

Once in business for herself in 1903 at the age of 31, Julia Morgan proved to be a perfectionist who put in 14-hour days, six days a week. Her office was relatively small with a staff of only 12, many of them female. Morgan believed in being involved with each commission from the first client-architect interview, to providing initial drawings, overseeing apprentices and draftsman and inspecting the work site.

She shunned publicity, had little social life, and never married. She was awarded many commissions, and women were among her greatest patrons. An early and influential supporter of Morgan was Phoebe Apperson Hearst, mother of Morgan's other great patron, William Randolph Hearst. Morgan's success at this time is all the more remarkable because she was a woman and prejudice against female architects was widespread. But her skill,

El Campanile, 1904, is an important centerpiece on the Mills College campus in Oakland, California.

professionalism, and talent overcame bias against her, and she continued to work until she closed her office at the age of 78.

No job was ever too small for Morgan, because she felt that larger commissions often came from smaller ones. This was certainly the case during Morgan's career, and she worked tirelessly to establish her reputation as an architect of churches, schools, women's clubs, institutional buildings, and at least 20 houses a year. Exact numbers are hard to determine, but records show that by the time she retired, she had drawings for over 1,000 buildings and had worked on between 600 and 800 structures, additions, and alterations.

Art historian Richard Longstreth characterizes her style as "Simplicity, order and restraint", as reflected in buildings constructed of unadorned elements and plain materials such as stucco and red cedar so popular in California. She liked historical styles: Mission, Spanish Colonial Revival, Arts and Crafts, Prairie, and even Renaissance Revival and often combined different elements from more than one to create an interest-

Julia Morgan wore pants under her long skirts so that she could climb up ladders, walk across scaffolding, and inspect her construction sites.

ing look. She preferred arches, large window areas, exposed structural beams, and painted tile. Above all, when possible, materials came from the local environment to achieve as close a harmony with nature as possible. Morgan insisted on excellence in craftsmanship without unnecessary fuss and lavishness. This she learned from Maybeck and the Arts and Crafts style he advocated.

Upon her return to California from Paris, Morgan worked for a short time with the architect John Galen Howard. She soon grew impatient to be on her own and in 1903 received a commission from Mr. and Mrs. F.M. Smith, owners of the Borax Soap Company, to design a campanile or bell tower, at Mills College in Oakland, California. Mills was a women's college and the first of many commissions throughout her career that would be for a women's institution.

El Campanile was located on a grassy oval shaded by live oaks and eucalyptus trees. It was designed to house 10 bells that had been cast in 1893 for exhibition at the World's Columbian Exposition in Chicago and shown the following year at the San Francisco Mid-Winter Fair. In 1902, the bells were given as a gift to Mills, to be hung in Morgan's beautiful bell tower. The campanile was dedicated on April 14, 1904.

The commission for the Mills Library came next and was built between 1905-1906. Both the campanile and library withstood the terrible San Francisco earthquake of 1906. This above all else established Morgan's reputation as a skilled engineer and architect, and over the next decade she designed many more buildings for the Mills campus including the gymnasium in 1910 (demolished in 1960) and the Alumnae House in 1916 (now the Student Union).

Morgan's "earthquake-proof" buildings for Mills College soon led to a major commission: the renovation of the famous Fairmont Hotel in San Francisco, ruined in the 1906 catastrophe. Burnt and crumbling, Morgan had to replace and strengthen structural beams and columns. But this kind of work demanded on-site supervision, which at the time was unheard of for a woman. The then fashionable long skirts and high stiff collars made it nearly impossible for Morgan to trek through shards of glass, fallen timber, and piles of ash, much less climb a ladder or walk across a beam. And so Morgan wore pants under her skirt and went freely about her business!

The Fairmont assignment is important in Morgan's career because a difficult engineering job was given to a woman instead of a man, and because it dealt with the issue of preservation of a fine building. Morgan answered questions by a reporter, who, of course thought she was only the interior designer, "I don't think you understand just what my work here has been. The decorative part was all done by a New York firm . . . my work has been structural." Upon the completion of the Fairmont assignment, Morgan's career as an architect of the highest caliber was formally established.

Morgan's first major benefactor Phoebe Hearst helped her obtain many important commissions from the YWCA. The Young Woman's Christian Association was founded in Boston in 1866 to help women who came to the city needing work and a place to live. Chapters were soon formed in cities across the nation. Hearst was a strong supporter of this organization and suggested Morgan as an architect for the National YWCA summer conference center at Asilomar, California, on the Pacific Ocean. Morgan designed everything for that project, including the entrance gates, the roads, buildings, and the large sleeping tents that could accommodate 350 women. Morgan designed the whole camp around a circle, using local materials to blend in with the redwoods and Monterey pines. The buildings, for the most part, are simple and horizontal in conception. The first structure built, and still in use today, was the Phoebe Apperson Hearst Administration Building.

Among the most impressive of the YWCA buildings was Merrill Hall completed in 1928. A large rectangular space capable of seating 1,000 people,

Morgan designed many buildings for the YWCA during her career. Merill Hall, Conference Center at Asilomar, California, 1928, was her first major commission for this organization.

The Asilomar Gates were designed by Morgan.

Tent House at Asilomar, 1913–1917.

the building was constructed of wood and stone, with an emphasis on large windows. The structural elements of the building were in clear view with exposed timbers, brass nuts and screws, and lighting fixtures on display. The unpainted wood was stenciled with sea horses and shells to recall the water nearby. The hall was built on a slight incline and rose above the skyline of Asilomar as tall and proud as the cedars that surrounded it. By working in harmony with nature and leaving the materials in their natural state, Morgan created a piece of architecture at one with the environment.

Other important YWCA commissions followed in Oakland, San Diego, Berkeley, Palo Alto, and San Jose in California and in Hawaii. Morgan enjoyed such great success with the YWCA that in 1918 they asked her to assume the position of staff architect. Unwilling to move to the Midwest and preferring to work on a variety of commissions, she declined the offer.

Morgan's greatest accomplishment, of course, was to be the complex of buildings at San Simeon, California built between 1919-1947. Employed by publishing magnate William Randolph Hearst to design what he described as something "simple" and sort of like a "bungalow," Morgan created what can only be described as a castle.

Plot plan of San Simeon.

The plan eventually included the main house, Casa Grande, and three smaller guest houses with an exterior pool, interior pool, and expansive grounds to accommodate formal gardens, outbuildings, and all sorts of outdoor activities. The style of architecture on the "Enchanted Hill" as Hearst called it, was Spanish Colonial Revival with stucco, colored decorative tile, arches, wrought iron, balconies and red tile roofs. It housed an art collection that included banners from Sienna, Italy, choir stalls from Spanish churches, painted Gothic windows, and all sorts of priceless European paintings and sculpture.

Casa Grande is spectacular. Organized in an I-shape, the bottom half is a small foyer leading into an enormous long assembly hall. The ceilings were imported from Spain and are magnificently decorated; large tapestries and old choir stalls run the length of the walls. An immense fireplace is located midway in the room, and doors on either side lead to the gracious dining room that can seat 40 people. The top of the "I" has a smaller dining room.

But Casa Grande was not big enough for Hearst. He wanted an even larger castle with another wing containing a kitchen and servants' quarters. He

William R. Hearst's compound at San Simeon in California occupied Morgan from 1919–1947 and was her greatest challenge and accomplishment. Here is the Casa Grande, or main house, where Hearst stayed.

wanted an even bigger assembly hall! Morgan's beautiful drawings and blueprints were covered with his notes. No matter what her private thoughts, Morgan kept them to herself, and Hearst always got his way. He could afford to make whatever changes he wanted.

To be a guest at San Simeon was to be treated to marvelous dinner parties, costume balls, and first-run movies in a private movie theater. In this setting, Hearst was called "the Chief" and San Simeon simply "the ranch." The author Ludwig Bemelmans wrote about the dining hall: "I walked through the dining hall . . . [there] is a table the length of the room, so big that whoever sits at the far end is very small. [There] is a fireplace that devours the trunks of trees . . . There are tall candlesticks all along the center of the long refectory table, and between them stand, in a straight line and in repeating pattern, bottles of catsup, chili sauce, pickled peaches, A-1 Sauce, salt and pepper in shakers that are cute little 5-and-10 cent figures of Donald Duck with silvered porcelain feet, and glasses in which are stuck a handful of paper napkins."

Hearst was very wealthy and equally willful, often deciding to change elements of the Castle after they had already been built. He demanded, for example, that a completed fireplace be moved from one side of the room to the other . . . and then back again. These renovations cost thousands and thousands of dollars and much inconvenience, but he wanted things done his way! Morgan worked 10 to 12 hours a day often getting no more than a few hours sleep at night, because to reach San Simeon she rode the train for six hours, then had a three hour taxi ride on top of that. She would leave San Francisco and arrive just in time to have breakfast with Hearst.

San Simeon took over 20 years to complete, and including all the artwork, cost approximately $5 million to build and furnish. In the 1950s, after Hearst's death, San Simeon became a California State Park, and is the second most widely visited attraction in California after Disneyland.

Morgan became ill at the age of 60, in 1932, with a recurrence of a childhood ear inflection. Operations left her paralyzed on one side of her face, and her retreat from public life became even more pronounced. Hearst cut back the work at San Simeon during the Great Depression of the 1930s. But he had another project in Northern California to which he turned most of his attention. On 65,000 acres near Mount Shasta along the banks of the McCloud River, Hearst built a rugged retreat. Earlier, Bernard Maybeck had designed a home for Phoebe Apperson Hearst, but it caught fire and burned. Hearst became enthralled with the idea of building amidst the forest, mountains, and rivers that reminded him so much of Germany. And so, he and Morgan settled on a Bavarian theme.

To aid in her research (and as a gift for her long-time commitment and friendship), Hearst sent Morgan to tour Europe via private car for several months. Work began on the Wyntoon complex as soon as she returned.

In its own way, Wyntoon was as elaborate and time-consuming a project as San Simeon, and Morgan's involvement on the project lasted from 1924 into the 1940s. Wyntoon became another playground for Heart's guests. Nearly impossible to reach by car, Hearst built a small airstrip there in the 1930s to make travel easier. Entertainment included nature hikes, horseback riding, croquet, swimming, and movies. It was far more rural than San Simeon, but in some ways more to Hearst's liking.

Wyntoon was arranged along the river with three main houses, each three stories high, clustered in what was called the Bavarian Village. Natural stone, timber, steep gables, and bay windows were charming and well suited to the setting. As with all her commissions, Morgan's craftsmen accompanied her, and the painting, sculpting, and woodwork combined to make the whole into a picture-perfect place.

Morgan so loved it there that it is said she did not want to be paid for her work, but only wanted to see it finished. In 1943, construction slowed down considerably, and Morgan left Wyntoon to work on other projects.

Late in Morgan's career, her balance became less steady and more than once she fell from a scaffold at Wyntoon. At the end of World War II, Hearst's fortunes again improved and he wanted Morgan to resume work at San Simeon, but at the age of 73 she was simply too tired. In 1951, after leaving

San Simeon and moving to Los Angeles, Hearst died of a heart attack. Morgan, who had been slowly reducing her workload in the 1940s finally called it quits in the summer of 1950. She contacted all her clients and asked them if they wanted drawings of their building from her files. Then, other than a few she saved for herself, she burned the rest. In failing health, she moved in with her sister's family where she lived until her death at the age of 85.

Julia Morgan achieved a great deal during her lifetime, not by introducing revolutionary designs or ideas but by executing quality work. Supported by women, she was in turn supportive of them and their causes. Morgan became a mentor for the many female architects that followed her lead. She never sought the limelight, but nonetheless established her place in a traditionally male profession.

In an interview with Marcia Mead, architect, in *The Christian Science Monitor* in November 27, 1931, Julia Morgan as said: "I think it is too early to say what contribution women are making in the field of architecture. They have as clients contributed very largely except, perhaps, in monumental buildings . . . . They have, however, done sincere good work along with the tide, and as the years go on, undoubtedly some greater than other architects will be developed, and in fair proportion to the number of outstanding men to the number in the rank and file."

LUDWIG MIES VAN DER ROHE

(1886-1969)

"Less is more."

—Mies van der Rohe

Mies van der Rohe shared the world architecture platform with Frank Lloyd Wright, Le Corbusier, and Walter Gropius as they charted the course of twentieth-century modern architecture. Mies' innovative design talent respected structure, proportions, details and materials above all else. Although many designers tried to imitate Mies' skyscrapers, they lacked his sense of style and purist view of architecture that made his works complete, and as some said, nearly perfect. The fact that others copied Mies' style but could not capture his sense of beauty in their buildings proved Mies' statement that "simplicity isn't so simple."

Born to a stonemason in Aachen, Germany, in 1886, Mies had hands-on experience with the tools of the architectural trade almost from birth. His only formal education was at the Cathedral School in Aachen, followed by trade school at age 13. He learned the basics of classical architecture by being an apprentice to a local draftsman of stucco ornament until the age of 19. With a good grounding in masonry and brickwork acquired from his father, plus what he had learned in trade school and as an apprentice, he left his hometown for Berlin and was hired by Bruno Paul, a leading German furniture designer.

In 1907, Mies landed his first independent commission, the Riehl House. It proved to be an attractive building, especially in light of Mies' age and relative inexperience. But he knew he needed more training, and in 1908, he became an apprentice to Peter Behrens, an industrial architect and one of the most advanced and forward-thinking designers in Germany. Factories were Behrens' specialty; in his most famous commission, the A.E.G. Turbine Factory in Berlin, 1909, he used modern technology to create a stunning architectural statement.

Mies was heavily influenced by Behrens, especially his interest in neo-classical architecture and its application in Behrens' own work. Critic Peter Blake has identified three major trends in Mies' work that stem from this classical interest that were repeated over and over again in his designs: a preference for a formal "base", situating buildings on wide platforms to set them apart; a keen regard for proportion and scale regardless of the type of building; and a feeling for structural materials and their relationship to the way the building looks, which Mies refined throughout his career.

Mies was assigned to an engineering regiment for the duration of World War I. In 1919, he became vocal as a member of the Novembergruppe, a politically active group of artists and designers who organized exhibitions and published their opinions in the magazine *Gestalung*, where Mies was able to express some of his design ideas. He developed a unique way of presenting his work through a combination of classical drawings and photomontage. In other words, he photographed drawings of a building and placed them on pictures of the site as it actually would appear when built. Mies received many commissions based upon his clear proposals.

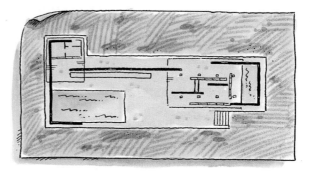

Floorplan sketch of German Pavilion in Barcelona, Spain, 1929.

In 1926, Mies became the first vice president of the Deutcher Werkbund, a group founded in 1907, to promote good design by leading architects, artists, and industrialists to German manufacturers. This was the only form of advertisement available to these gifted artisans at this time. Mies organized a major exhibition of the Werkbund in Stuttgart, Germany, in 1927, which featured modern buildings. The finest architects in Europe were commissioned to design a group of low-rise freestanding buildings in the city of Stuttgart. The roster included Gropius, Le Corbusier, J. J. P. Oud, Peter Behrens, Hans Scharous, and Mies, all of whom were contributors to this important project.

Mies' design for the German Pavilion for the International Exhibition at Barcelona, Spain in 1929 was his greatest European accomplishment. In this one-story structure, he introduced the beginning of his simple and sophisticated design concepts that followed the "less is more" theory. The building, raised upon a slab of travertine marble, a white porous stone, was a complex arrangement of vertical and horizontal planes. It was a temporary structure for the fair and few architects saw it, but it is well known through photographs and acclaim.

Mies used sumptuous materials for the pavilion—marble, chrome, and water—and he designed the furniture inside. The famous Barcelona Chair

Mies' Barcelona Chair, 1926, and MR Chair, 1929, are among the most sophisticated and beautiful pieces of furniture ever designed.

was made of a supporting steel frame in the shape of an "X" with leather strips stretched lengthwise across the cantilevered seat and up the back to support the leather cushions. Even today this chair is considered as one of the most beautiful pieces of furniture designed in the twentieth century.

Mies also created the MR chair during this period. The masterful French designer Marcel Breuer was simultaneously working on a similar design he called the Wassily armchair. Both depended upon bent steel tubing as a frame. The seat and back were of leather or cane and the contrast of modern steel and natural materials was stunning. The chair could be reconfigured as a stool or reclining sofa (the design principle of the Barcelona chair was also applied to coffee tables or sofas) but most importantly, the MR chair could be mass produced.

The design and placement of furniture in Mies' buildings were, for him, the way to balance and complete his designs. His chairs and tables worked well as independent objects or grouped together in a lobby or living room usually arranged upon a square rug. His interior designs were never fussy or cluttered, and only occasionally included sculpture, plants or flowers for decoration.

S.R.Crown Hall, Illinois Institute of Technology, Chicago, Illinois, 1950–1958.

Mies became Director of the Bauhaus School in 1930, the year it was moved to Berlin. In 1931, Hitler closed the program and soon thereafter Mies left Germany for America at the invitation of architect Philip Johnson. He settled in Chicago in 1938, and was appointed director of Chicago's Armour Institute, now the Illinois Institute of Technology. During his 20 year tenure there, Mies was responsible for not only all academic programs but for planning the campus and designing many of its buildings: the library, the administrative building, the chapel and S. R. Crown Hall. All these buildings followed Mies' design preference of a steel frame with glass or yellow brick panels for infill. Later, other architects (with varying degrees of skill and talent) added to the campus and altered this plan.

S.R.Crown Hall, built 1950-1958, was one of Mies' last and best building designs for the Illinois Institute of Technology. It is a single-story structure resting on a white marble podium, with no interior supports thus resulting in a large interior space. The roof is upheld by four massive steel plates, which are carried by eight exterior steel columns spaced 60 feet apart. Glass

The apartments at 860–880 Lake Shore Drive in Chicago, Illinois, designed by Mies between 1948–1951, remain among his most attractive and influential high-rise designs.

plates enclose the building from floor to ceiling. The spacious interior is subdivided by free-standing wall partitions. Two stairways lead to the basement area where additional classrooms and service facilities are located.

Following his successful career at the Illinois Institute of Technology, Mies was offered many important commissions. First among them was the 860–880 Lake Shore Drive Apartments, highly visible along Chicago's Lake Michigan shore. Mies' contribution to skyscraper design, which had not really shown much progress since the 1930s, was as significant as the contributions made by Louis Sullivan. It was through his evolution of steel frame construction that buildings such as these high-rise apartments were built, and today are seen in cities all over America.

The Chicago fire code dictated that all structural steel work be covered by a minimum of two inches of concrete. Faced with this restriction, Mies came up with a brilliant solution that did not compromise his architectural design. The steel skeleton was sheathed in fireproof casing according to the law, and then a second steel skeleton was hung on the building to give the illusion that, in fact, it was the only steel frame of the building. In other words, the actual core of the building was not visible, and what was visible was decorative but mimicked the real skeleton. Mies girdled the building in welded I-beams hung in a vertical and horizontal grid. The corner columns were strengthened by sheet steel, which was also applied to the I-beams. The steel work was painted black and the windows were tinted.

The two 26-story towers were identical and placed perpendicular to each other. The first floor of glass walls were recessed behind a continuous row of black columns. Travertine marble slabs, upon which the buildings rested, and a continuous cantilevered canopy connected the two towers. Parking was located underground. All elevators, stairways, and mechanical services for the buildings were placed in the center of the apartments; kitchens and bathrooms were located nearby, making the all glass exterior possible. The enormous success of these towers set the precedent for Mies' greatest landmark, the Seagram Building in New York City.

Erected in the business district on the most expensive real estate in Manhattan, the Seagram Building at 375 Park Avenue in New York City, 1958, was Mies' masterwork. He collaborated on this project with Philip Johnson, who was primarily responsible for the sumptuous interior, especially that of the famous Four Seasons Restaurant. Commissioned by the daughter of the Seagram family, Mies erected a 39-story tower that was the most costly office building of its time. Employing the same technique for fireproof casing he had incorporated in the Lake Shore Drive Apartments, Mies used an exterior structure of bronze and a curtain of bronze-tinted glass windows. The building stands 90 feet from Park Avenue and covers 25 percent of its lot area. This allowed Mies to include a large plaza in front of the entrance, framed on either side by pools with fountains, groves of trees, and benches of serpentine marble. The pavement was of pink granite that extended into the lobby, and a canopy over the door directed visitors to the entrance. The glass walls of the lobby were set back behind bronze columns.

The spine of the building at the rear contained all mechanical services and was flanked by two smaller wings.

The Seagram Building, which received the American Institute of Architect's 25 Year Award in 1984, is as close to perfection in plan and detail as Mies could achieve. It was imitated by other architects, but they never could capture Mies' handsome artistry. He was able to imbue seemingly cold, impersonal materials with life and sensitivity. He was able to create beauty and allow the building to function with seemingly very few extras. His own words best sum up his views on the future of architectural design: "I am convinced that traditional methods of building will disappear. In any case anyone regrets that the house of the future can no longer be made by hand workers, it should be borne in mind that the automobile is no longer manufactured by carriage makers."

Seagram Building, New York City, 1954–1958.

The Farnsworth House in Plano, Illinois, built in 1945-1950, illustrates how Mies' modern building practices could be used for skyscraper and private home alike. Built as a weekend retreat on the edge of the Fox River, the glass house is built as a steel rectangle. Mies used his favored slab travertine floor in white marble, this time raised above flood level; eight exterior steel

The Farnsworth House, Plano, Illinois, 1945–50.

columns set 22 feet apart provided support for both the elevated floor and the roof. The walls are all of glass, except for the screened-in porch. Wood paneling was used for partitions, and the steel frame was painted white. Privacy was achieved by hanging white silk curtains at the windows.

Unfortunately, the owner of the house, Dr. Edith Farnsworth, was so displeased with what has been considered by many as one of Mies' greatest designs, that she sued Mies for damages. He won the lawsuit, but he never would discuss it. Today, the ill-begotten Farnsworth residence, once set on 75 acres of wooded land, is crowded by road construction and a bridge over the Fox River.

Many honors and medals were awarded Mies during his career: in 1959, the Gold Medal of the Royal Institute of British Architecture, in 1960, the Gold

Medal of the American Institute of Architects, and in 1966, the Gold Medal from the Institute of German Architects. Perhaps most meaningful to Mies, however, was when President John F. Kennedy gave him the Presidential Medal of Freedom in 1963 for his contribution to architecture and impact as one of the leading post-war designers in the United States. This particular honor confirmed Mies' reputation among his peers and gained him recognition from the public he served.

The contribution of Mies van der Rohe to twentieth-century architecture is tremendous and the path architecture would have taken without his influence is unimaginable to his followers. His ability to make a personal artistic statement out of metal and glass can only be seen when his work is compared to lesser architects. Architect Eero Saarinen, a contemporary, captured the essence of this best when he said in the dedication of Mies' S. R. Crown Hall in 1956: "Great architecture is both universal and individual . . . . The universality comes because there is an architecture expressive of its time. But the individuality comes as the expression of one man's unique combination of faith and honesty and devotion and belief in architecture—in short, his moral integrity."

PAUL R. WILLIAMS

(1894-1980)

"Remember that you are an American and that the last four letters of the word AMERICAN spell I CAN. And if you will combine the definition of progress with AMERICAN, you have the real formula for SUCCESS."

—Paul R. Williams

In order for Paul Revere Williams to become an architect in the early twentieth century, he had to believe that African-Americans could, should, and would rise above prejudice and prove their worth as individuals through courage and effort. His greatness lies in his ultimate success in being accepted as an architect who was judged for his talent, and not by the color of his skin. As a pioneer among African-American architects, he set an example for black men and women to follow.

Williams entered an architectural profession that was dominated by white Anglo-Saxon Protestant men. Few ethnic minorities, women, or immigrants attended the most prestigious New England ivy league schools that had architectural or engineering programs, much less the exclusive École des

Beaux-Arts in Paris. Further, nonwhite American men and white females were not admitted to the social world in which contact with affluent clients might be made and commissions arranged. Blacks, women, and immigrants also were barred from professional associations, such as the American Institute of Architects and the New York Architectural League.

The paradox of Paul Williams' success is illustrated by the fact that, by the 1940s, he could afford to build a beautiful house in the fanciest Los Angeles suburb, but was banned from that neighborhood by prejudice. He was known as an "architect to the stars," including Frank Sinatra, Barbara Stanwyck, Betty Grable, Cary Grant, and many others, but he rarely attended their parties or socialized with them. Paul and his wife Della, instead, kept company with other gifted black men and women of their day: singer Lena Horne, congressman Adam Clayton Powell, dancer Bill "Bojangles" Robinson, the NAACP's (National Association for the Advancement of Colored People) Walter White and Nancy Bethume, and Olympic star Jesse Owens.

Williams was not bitter about his situation, but chose to see himself as a "Negro" professional, and played whatever part he could in the civil rights movement. And he arrived at the top of his career based on merit.

In 1926, Paul Williams was admitted to the Los Angeles Chapter of the American Institute of Architects, and in 1956, 30 years later, he became the first black nominated to the AIA College of Fellows.

Williams benefited by the World War II economic boom, which had a dramatic impact on the future of black architects in general in America. Millions of dollars of government commissions during the war went to the African-American firm of McKissack and McKissack, Hilyard Robinson, and Paul Williams. In addition, loans and scholarship money became available for education; and while some universities were still segregated, many blacks attended fine institutions such as Howard University, the Tuskegee Institute, and Hampton College. Howard's architecture program was accredited in 1950, and a large number of black architects graduated from there eventually to set up practices in the Washington, D.C. area.

Williams was born in 1894 in Los Angeles, and orphaned at age four. Raised by a foster mother and brought up in the African Methodist Episcopal Church, Williams attended the neighborhood schools and soon showed a tremendous talent for drawing. Early, he declared an interest in architecture, only to be discouraged by his teachers who could not imagine Williams ever attracting enough clients to stay in business.

But Williams was determined to become an architect. From 1913 to 1916, he attended the Los Angeles wing of the Beaux-Arts Institute. His first real job was with urban planner and landscape architect William D. Cook. Cook specialized in designing private homes, public parks, suburban communities, and city plans. During Williams' time with the firm, 1914–1916, the office designed a new town, Planada; and gardens for the W.L. Dodge home in Los Angeles built by architect Irving Gill.

Williams took time out to enroll in the University of South Carolina School of Engineering until 1919, and although he did not graduate, he improved his skills in this area. Also, while in Cook's office, he submitted an entry in the competition sponsored by the Pasadena City Commission for a modest suburban center with public park, small shopping center, public buildings and an apartment complex. He won first prize and $200.

Like most young architects, Williams recognized the value of working under an established designer. So he next moved to the office of Reginald D. Johnson, a residential architect in southern California. Johnson preferred a mix between Craftsmen and Spanish Mediterranean styles. Many small homes and country houses were designed when Williams was in Johnson's office, and for the rest of his career Williams would be recognized primarily as a residential architect.

During this time, Williams won yet another competition for a bungalow design with formal garden. One of the judges was John C. Austen, a commercial builder of office buildings, industrial plants, apartments, and civic centers. In 1919, Williams jumped at the chance to work for Austen, to learn about the art of building "big" structures as well as learning about the application of new styles. Two years later, Williams passed his state architectural exam in 1921, left Austen, and received his license to practice a year later. Records indicate that by 1924 he had started his own practice.

To open his own practice and expect clients, especially wealthy, white clients was a brave and risky thing for Williams to do. He placed a large ad in the telephone book, and when new customers arrived at his door and saw a black man, many were taken aback. To overcome their discomfort, Williams persuaded some to stay and offered a free consultation on their project. To keep his clients comfortable, Williams sat opposite them and drew upside down to ensure a "safe" distance between them. His manners, complimentary advice and talent brought him the business he desired. In addition he had left Austen with over six commissions, five for middle-income homes in or near Los Angeles—so he had his start.

His earliest houses were designed in the Mediterranean style, often single-story ranches with low-pitched red tile roofs, shutters, and porches to provide outdoor living space. His interiors were comfortable with rooms coming off hallways.

The beautiful E.L Cord Residence of 1931 was typical of the glamorous Beverly Hills houses that Williams designed for the wealthy and famous.

In the 1930s, he received the commission that would make his career: the E.L. Cord House, in Beverly Hills, California. Mr. Cord, the chairman of Cord-Auburn Automobiles wanted a family mansion built on an eight-and-one-half acre lot. Other architects had been asked for their ideas but the soonest they could deliver preliminary plans and elevations was a minimum of two to three weeks. Given an opportunity to talk with Mr. Cord, Williams convinced him that he could provide working drawings the next afternoon. Skeptical, Mr. Cord agreed. Williams wrote about the Cord house later in his book, *I Am a Negro*, "I delivered those preliminary plans by the sched-uled hour—but I did not tell him that I had worked for 22 hours, without sleeping or eating."

The completed home was enormous, containing 16 bedrooms and 22 painted bathrooms, complete with 14-carat gold and sterling silver fixtures. Borrowing from the Southern Colonial style, the painted white brick main block was accented by a two-story portico on thin columns. The shuttered windows, classical detailing of doorways, balcony and ornamentation came together to give the house a majestic look well suited to its nickname Cord Haven. The relative simplicity of the exterior contrasted with the opulent Georgian and French detailing of the interior. This house, more than any other, established Williams as a Hollywood architect. Sadly, in 1962, the house was dismantled by developers, and the furnishings and building materials sold.

The pool of the Jay Paley Residence in Holmby Hills, California, 1934, was spectacular with its oval shape and curving, colorful Art Deco design.

Another mansion Williams designed around this time, and very much in the same glamorous Hollywood tradition, was the Jay Paley Residence built in Holmby Hills section of Los Angeles in 1934. Here the look was more modern, with metal used for Art Deco detailing and a wonderful curved two-story porch supported by slender columns. Classical touches such as round arched windows and doorways with triangular pediments above them were included, but the feeling was fresh and beautiful.

Williams' business flourished in the 1930s as Los Angeles began to recover from the Great Depression. Business was also booming in the motion picture, oil, and defense manufacturing industries. Williams designed more than 22 homes in one year, many of them mansions or country houses. The majority of these houses were designed in the Georgian or Regency styles; always gracious and elegant but never overly concerned with classical detailing.

Williams enjoyed the interplay between interior and exterior spaces, and whenever possible, would include large glass areas that showcased a beautiful garden beyond. Williams used curves as a main design feature, and nowhere were they more prominently displayed than in his magnificent staircases. Here, upon entry, was where home owners wanted to introduce their exquisite residences: the vestibules and winding staircases designed by Williams were indeed special. Most important, Williams' houses

A signature curving staircase in the Paul R. Williams' Residence, Los Angeles, California, 1951.

were livable. No matter how grand or how small they were comfortable family homes that suited the inhabitants. This was a major factor in Williams' popularity.

In the late 1930s and 1940s, Williams started to receive the sort of commissions he had longed for: major commercial and civic projects. Williams was chosen to design the interior of the Beverly Hills Saks Fifth Avenue department store in 1939, a plum commission.

The comfortable, sophisticated, living room–like–feeling was just what Saks Fifth Avenue wanted from Williams in this 1939 Beverly Hills, California showroom.

The feeling Saks wanted to create for its customers was of being in someone's home; a comfortable, low-key yet sophisticated approach to merchandising. Williams, the residential architect, fit the bill. He introduced soft indirect lighting by using small spotlights for display cases and other sales areas. A silky surface paint produced a velvet like surface that kept reflection to a minimum and gave a rich look to the surroundings. Mirrors were treated as picture frames, and small paintings adorned the walls. In short, Williams changed the look of the department store, made it more home-like and set a precedent for other designers.

Williams also held the post of Commissioner of National Board of Municipal Housing from 1933 to 1941. During this period, he designed a major public housing project, Pueblo del Rio in southeast Los Angeles. This 400-unit apartment complex housed 1,350 people. Williams was chief architect for

The Fountain Coffee Shop in the Beverly Hills Hotel of 1947–1951 was the talk of the town with its curving countertop, bar chairs and exotic Don Loper designed palm leaf wallpaper.

this and many other projects he worked on with a number of other established architects. Of the fifteen public housing projects built by the Municipal Housing Board during Williams' tenure, only Pueblo del Rio was open to African-Americans.

Between 1947 and 1951, Williams completed one of his most famous projects, the Beverly Hills Hotel. His designs for the Polo Lounge, Fountain Coffee Shop, and alterations and additions for the Crescent Wing were the epitome of glamour, and helped reestablish the hotel as a fashionable resort. Particularly famous is the curved countertop of the Fountain Restaurant and the palm leaf wallpaper (designed by Don Loper) which suggested an indoor/outdoor feeling. Recently, the hotel has undergone a multimillion-dollar renovation, which maintained the spirit and form of Paul Williams' interiors.

Through all his success and dealings with wealthy clients, Paul Williams never forgot the needs of the average middle-class American. World War II veterans wanting their own houses could turn to his books: *The Small Home of Tomorrow* (1945); and *New Homes for Today* (1946) to find patterns for houses that were attractive and affordable. Using new materials and technologies, with his usual preference for classical styling, clean lines, and even gardens, Williams' books made the American dream of owning a home a reality for many. All home owners had to do was select the plan that best suited their needs, hire a contractor, buy the lot to put it on, acquire the materials, and for $3,000 to $10,000, they had a new house!

By the late 1940s, Williams office was receiving architectural commissions for clients in Mexico and Bogota, Columbia. He also continued to serve on California boards and national commissions, the latter at the request of presidents Franklin Delano Roosevelt and Dwight D. Eisenhower.

Paul Williams believed that traditional architecture would long outlast more trendy styles. Reflected in his work is a deep concern for family traditions, comfort, beauty, and a respect for materials. But for all his conservatism in building, Paul Williams remained a true activist in civil rights. He never stopped believing in himself as an individual and his right to success. In this he was a leader for other black and minority architects to follow.

PHILIP JOHNSON

(b. 1906)

"I'm not creating forms; I'm creating attitudes."

—Philip Johnson

It is difficult to describe all that is Philip Johnson. He is an architecture critic, an architect, a museum curator, a commentator, and a trendsetter. He has been called the dean of contemporary architects because, for the past 60 years, he has set the pace for architectural change. The partnership of Philip Johnson and John Burgee that flowered in the 1970s and 1980s unquestionably resulted in the creation of some of the most innovative and beautiful structures ever built. Their touch was magic: the buildings for corporate American that they designed, and those that they influenced, changed skylines in almost every major city. Johnson, still active in semi-retirement, maintains his keen wit, fertile imagination, and untiring interest that have kept him designing, writing, and contributing to the world of architecture.

Johnson was born in 1906 to a wealthy lawyer and his wife in Cleveland, Ohio. The financial security his father offered gave him the freedom to pursue any career that interested him. At Harvard, as an undergraduate, he studied classics and philosophy. After graduation in 1930, he befriended the architectural historian and critic Henry-Russell Hitchcock, and together they traveled to Europe investigating the new architecture there. Upon his return in 1932, he became the first director of the Department of Architecture and Design at the Museum of Modern Art. He was to remain involved with the museum throughout his career, filling the director's position twice, serving as a trustee, and donating a large number of modern artworks from his private collection.

It was at this time, in 1932, that Johnson and Henry-Russell Hitchcock staged an exhibit and co-wrote the book *The International Style: Architecture Since 1922*. The exhibit and book showcased modern European architecture with its sleek lines, geometric shapes, and flush windows. This style became known as the International Style.

Johnson traveled again to Europe during the 1930s, this time visiting Germany and acquainting himself with architects Walter Gropius, Le Corbusier, and Mies van der Rohe—all of them intricately tied to the Bauhaus School of Design in Dessau, Germany, and its modern ideas. Johnson was instrumental in luring many of the famous European architects to America. In 1937, Walter Gropius, former principal of the Bauhaus, became chairman of the Harvard Design School. In 1937, Mies van der Rohe, with whom Johnson was particularly friendly, came to America and eventually assumed the position of director of the Chicago Armour Institute School of Architecture later known as the Illinois Institute of Technology.

So taken was Johnson with design and structural technology that in 1941, he reentered Harvard to study design under Gropius and Marcel Breuer (also a member of the Bauhaus specializing in small homes and furniture). At 37 Johnson emerged as an architect. Shortly thereafter he was called to

Johnson's Glass House in New Canaan, Connecticut of 1949 redefined the meaning of residential privacy.

serve in World War II, and returned in 1946 to the Museum of Modern Art where he resumed his prior post.

In his early career in the 1950s and the 1960s, and even in some later projects, Johnson was heavily influenced by Mies, so much so that many criticized Johnson for simply copying his designs. But Johnson replied that mimickry was the greatest form of flattery and that he was acknowledging his debt to the great German master. Then in the 1970s and 1980s, Johnson turned toward "historicism," or architectural styles of the past that allowed little room for Mies' modernism. From this point on, the rise in his career was meteoric, due in part to his reputation as a respected critic, his outspokenness, and his important post at the museum.

Johnson's first designs were for small houses, with the exception of his collaboration with Mies on the Seagram Building in New York City which was finished in 1958.

In 1949, Johnson designed the Glass House in New Canaan, Connecticut as his personal residence. It was intended from the start as a home for one person, and it redefined the meaning of privacy with its glass walls. It has a large single room (32' X 56') that rests on a brick platform. At the center is a large round chimney of red brick that houses, on one side, restroom facilities, and, on the other side, a fireplace. All four glass walls are symmetrical with a door in the center of each. A steel frame and a "chair rail" of thin steel that encircles the house holds it all together. Nearby on the property is a brick guest house and sculpture garden. Over the years, Johnson has added other structures (one which we will address later) to this residential compound.

By design, the Glass House is concealed from the public road. A solid brick wall forces the visitor to approach by a series of 45-degree turns. Johnson is very concerned about the "processional" aspect of architecture, and he wanted to control the way guests approach and enter his home. This is how he maintains his privacy even with a completely transparent house.

The Glass House has often been compared to the glass Farnsworth House designed by Mies. Although not completed until two years after Johnson's home, Mies' work was begun first, and Johnson was well acquainted with it. Within the one-room house, Johnson designed areas for certain activities, suggested by the arrangement of furniture. A walnut storage cabinet, for example, hides the bedroom and the study on the side. Trees and shrubbery provide natural "curtains" and "wallpaper": the home is transparent and full of reflections at the same time.

The Glass House and the Seagram Building were Johnson's tribute to Mies' severe International Style. Then Johnson did an architectural about-face in 1967 when he joined forces with John Burgee (b. 1933). Together, they created the best work of their careers and changed the image of the skyscraper. Until their partnership, architects were wary of designing buildings on speculation, meaning that there was no guarantee that tenants could be found. But Johnson and Burgee built many buildings on that risky basis.

John Burgee with Philip Johnson created a unique look for corporate architecture.

Pennzoil Place in Houston, Texas, 1976, poses a striking silhouette against the downtown skyline.

"We never copy ourselves," said Johnson and Burgee of their stylistically diverse buildings. They had no trademark style that could be imitated, thus the spirit of change and spectacle was invigorating and all their contemporaries were aware of it. "Historicism" became their keyword, and with each new building, some tradition from the past was brought forward and used in an unexpected way.

An example of their collective creative genius was Pennzoil Place in Houston, Texas, built in 1976. One of several skyscraper projects put together by Texas developer, Gerald P. Hines, this project broke all real estate records by leasing 1.2 million square feet immediately. Twin bronze towers with bronze-tinted glass rise side by side, but are unexpectedly separated by a 10-foot gap. At first, they appear as a single unit but then the "processional" element of Johnson's work shows itself—the view changes upon approach. The buildings are trapezoidal with sharp slanted roofs pitched at 45 degrees. Banks, shops, and restaurants are all housed beneath two triangular glass roofs that fill the atriums with light.

Pennzoil Place dominated the Houston skyline for eight years, not because of its height but because of its unique design.

Televangelist, Reverend Dr. Robert M. Schuller, called upon Johnson and Burgee when he wanted to expand his current church and conduct his "Hour of Power" radio show in a setting big enough for 3,000 congregants. They delivered the Garden Grove Community Church, 1980, in Garden Grove, California.

This mirrored wonder-building is enormous, measuring 128 feet tall at its highest point, 415 feet long, and 207 feet wide. Based on the design of a Latin cross, the architects elongated it to focus all attention on the chancel where services are performed. The result is a four-pointed star with three balconies above the main floor for congregants and 90-foot doors that swing open during services to allow worshippers in their cars a glimpse of the interior while they listen to the service on the radio.

Garden Grove Community Church (Crystal Cathedral), Garden Grove, California, 1976–1980.

Splashing fountains line the center aisle and are turned off just before Schuller would speak. The church is covered with reflective glass that is supported by white trusses, or structural braces, forming an intricate web against the roof. Changes in the weather cause an other-worldly atmosphere within. Nature and spirit are wed here in a most unusual combination.

AT&T, the nation's largest telephone company described the conservative look it wanted in its new corporate headquarters in this way: "If we had one portrait painted, it should be by Norman Rockwell . . . If we were a U.S. General we would be Omar Bradley, not George Patton . . . If we were a tree, we would be a huge and utilitarian douglas fir, not a sequoia and certainly not a dogwood." In short, it wanted a building whose image was as solid and sincere as America itself. Johnson/Burgee Architects, in the skyscraper they designed in the shape of a Chippendale highboy, a piece of colonial American furniture, once again changed attitudes about what was trendy on Madison Avenue in New York City in the late 1970s and early 1980s. The expensive granite-clad building has 36 oversized stories. Following the highboy tradition, the floors of office space resemble a chest of "drawers" with a fanciful scroll on top resting on a stand 10-stories tall with slender columns or "legs" and an arch cut out of the center.

The design of the AT&T(American Telephone and Telegraph) Corporate Headquarters in New York City, 1984, draws its inspiration from American colonial furniture, the Chippendale highboy.

The spacious open air atrium at ground level provides a sheltered pedestrian area. A skylit galleria runs behind the tower while a three-story annex at ground level in the rear of the building is filled with shops and restaurants.

The AT&T Corporate Headquarters, completed in 1984, was the star of a movement called Post Modernism that pulled away from the severe geometry and stark glass and steel of the International Style. The building, if one looks carefully, is full of historic quotes from earlier buildings. For Johnson/Burgee Architects, historic architectural references became the rule, proving Johnson's statement, "We cannot not know history."

Johnson withdrew from the partnership with Burgee in 1987 to assume the role of consultant. He wanted time to work on his own projects, particularly his compound in New Canaan. Johnson had decided to give the now-famous home to the National Trust for Historic Preservation at the time of his death.

Therefore, a visitor's center would be required for its future use as a public museum. And who better to design it than Johnson himself.

"Monsta" is what he calls the black and red two-room sculptural form he built for that purpose in 1994-1995. It is one of his most personal creations. "Everytime I see this house, I pet it," Johnson told a critic with the *The New Yorker Magazine*.

Johnson's latest addition to his New Canaan, Connecticut compound is the architectural sculpture, Monsta, designed between 1994–1995.

Johnson designed the structure on computer. Its base is concrete sprayed on a wire mesh frame. The interior is off-white with one room for gifts and concessions and the other for viewing a video of Johnson's career—self-edited, of course. The corners are rounded, the ceiling height is 9 feet in one spot and 20 feet in another. Lighting is set into the floor. He said of the building: "The idea for this house has been coming for a long time . . . it's full of change and life and everything but straight lines. It's all intuitive. All wiggly. It hasn't any back and front and sides."

There is no way to pin Johnson down or make a definitive statement about his style or his opinions or his endless creative genius. His long career will, we hope, continue to give us even more architectural gifts and insights on the modern scene. He was awarded the Gold Medal from the American Institute of Architects in 1978 and the Pritzker Prize in Architecture in 1975. The public has been the recipient of the rest of Philip Johnson's awards.

IEOH MING PEI

(b. 1917)

"As artist - architects, the temptation is to give expression to every building we design. We tend to forget our greater responsibility to the whole — which is the street, the square, or the city itself."

—I.M. Pei

Whenever I.M. Pei is discussed, his concern for "urban regeneration"—giving new life to the neighborhood, community or city—is a primary topic. Pei does not think in terms of just the building he is currently designing but the role or impact that structure will have on the area surrounding it. He says, "Like people, buildings must exist in the context of their physical environment."

The challenge for Pei is not to create new environments, but to find a way to blend what is new with what is old. The passage of time in the cityscape, reflected in the history of building styles, is of particular interest to him.

Pei's designs are as diverse as his commissions. He has no one style. "I don't apply the same formula to all buildings." Pei says. "I start from scratch each time." He is consistent, however, in his preference for a precise and disciplined geometric order that appears complex at first glance, but that is ultimately orderly and understandable. His buildings are art forms—they must be experienced from outside to inside, first as single objects and then as part of a larger environment to be completely understood.

I. M. Pei was born into a wealthy banking family in Canton, China, in 1917. He spent his early childhood in the Orient and, in 1935, crossed the ocean to enroll at the Massachusetts Institute of Technology. Graduating five years later with a Bachelors of Architecture degree, he spent time traveling on a Massachusetts Institute of Technology Fellowship, working for an engineering firm, and volunteering for the National Defense Research Committee at Princeton. Homesick for his family, he longed to return to China, but his father cautioned him to stay in America where he would be safe during World War II. Pei married Eileen Loo just before entering Harvard School of Design in 1945. They have four children, two of whom have established their own practice. Pei earned his Master degrees in architecture in one year and stayed on to join the Harvard faculty.

A turning point in Pei's career was his alliance with the real estate firm of Webb and Knapp, from 1948 to 1955, where he was director of Architectural Research. William Zeckendorf was the mover and shaker of this real estate empire and he provided Pei with key commissions. These early works gave Pei a chance to hone his skills as a designer, planner, and developer, and especially gave him experience in what was to become his specialty: large projects.

Pei's partners, associates, and draftsmen worked as a team. Although he would oversee every project, each associate was responsible for a particular commission. In this way, Pei, along with others in his firm, were all part of

Denver Mile High Center, Denver, Colorado, 1956.

the planning, interior and exterior design, graphics, model making, and presentation for each job. The success of his firm depended on teamwork.

His first major commission from Webb and Knapp was for the Denver Mile High Center, in Denver, Colorado, 1956. What began as a 23-story office building evolved into a shopping/recreation complex. Pei added the May D & F Department Store in 1958, and the Denver Hilton in 1960. The May Department store had a large plaza in front, which Pei turned into a sunken skating rink in winter and an outdoor restaurant in summer. The office tower was built of steel and glass, while the Hilton was of reddish brown granite and tinted concrete, reflecting the Colorado mountains. Here was an early example of Pei's ability to unify buildings and create a workable and attractive urban space.

The year 1955 saw the development of I.M. Pei and Partners *Architects*, whose staff came mainly from Webb and Knapp. One of his most famous and infamous commissions at this time was the John Hancock Tower, 1976, Boston, Massachusetts. This 60-story, 2-million square foot tower occupied a block of the historic Copley Square District that also boasted such landmarks as Henry Hobson Richardson's Trinity Church and McKim, Mead, and White's Boston Public Library. How could such a modern building fit in?

The mirrored walls of the John Hancock Tower in Boston, Massachusetts, 1976, reflect the older buildings of historic Copley Square uniting the neighborhood in a unique and satisfying way.

Pei's solution was brilliant. The "parallelogram" tower was sheathed with reflective glass so that all surrounding buildings were mirrored on its surface. Instead of standing apart from the other buildings, it became, in Pei's unique fashion, part of the fabric of the neighborhood.

The John Hancock Building did have its share of structural problems though. In 1973, while under construction, a storm with high winds blew out one-third of the 10,000 glass windows, each one weighing 500 pounds.

National Gallery of Art, East Wing, Washington, D.C., 1978.

Until a solution was found, the missing windows were replaced with plywood boards and the building received the nickname "the tallest wooden building in the world." Ultimately, Henry Cobb, the principal designer, found a stronger and thicker glass pane replacement and reinforced the foundation of the 800-foot building to prevent this catastrophe from ever happening again. When the Hancock building received an award for excellence from the American Institute of Architects in 1977, one juror remarked, "It is perhaps the most handsome reflective glass building. History may show it to be the last example of the species."

Pei has been referred to many times as a "geometrist" or someone who bases his plans on geometric shapes and relationships. Such is the scheme of the magnificent East Wing of the National Gallery of Art in Washington, D.C., built in 1978. Erected directly across the street from John Pope's original National Gallery, the differences between the two are stunning and wonderful. Pei reinforces the relationship by cladding the new wing in the same marble from the same Tennessee quarry as Pope's original. There the similarities end!

The composition of the East Wing is based upon a series of large and small triangular shapes. An underground connecting link joins the new wing to the historic West Wing. The triangle is the unifying element that organizes the structure. The largest triangle, seven stories tall, houses the museum itself. Next door, a smaller structure is a study center for scholars and research. These two triangles flank yet another triangle with a magnificent glass ceiling that connects the other two. A red mobile by Alexander Calder dangles in the sunlight. This space is a fantastic surprise because of its height, openness and unusual shape. It is a central meeting place, and visitors move through it by means of walkways and a grand stairway to other parts of the gallery.

The clarity of design, the sharp corners and attention to technical detail make the East Wing a sculptural entity in itself. Because it is an unconventional museum space, however, it has been criticized as a show place for art, there are unusable corners and odd angular walls. But the gallery is compelling, and again Pei brought new life into an established district.

Geometrics also play an important part in the John F. Kennedy Library, completed in 1979, and situated in Columbia Harbor across from downtown Boston. This important commission, whose site is next to the water Kennedy loved so much, is a complex combination of rectangular solids, wedges, cylinders, and planes arranged in such a way that the exterior indicates nothing of the interior space and vice versa. In fact, once inside we are completely taken over by the exhibits, and the architecture becomes a container and a shepherd to guide us through JFK's presidency, marriage, and assassination with photographs, videos, political cartoons, clothes, and much more.

John Fitzgerald Kennedy Library and Museum, Boston, Massachusetts, 1979.

There are two auditoriums near the entrance with the principal exhibit space in the lower level. From this emotional, super-charged experience, Pei leads the visitor to perhaps one of his most awesome spaces: an enormous light-filled room looking seaward. There is no furniture here, only plants and a large American flag against one wall. This is a place for solitude, remembrance, and perhaps spiritual renewal.

"I told them you know, I'm not a fan. I'm really not. When I thought of rock and roll, all I thought of was my kids, and with me it was always 'Kids turn it down! Turn it down!' But the people on the committee said it didn't matter that I wasn't yet a fan . . . so I started my musical education." This was I.M. Pei's response to being asked to design the Rock and Roll Hall of Fame and Museum in Cleveland, Ohio in 1995. And yet all agree that the match between the modern "geometrist" and Americana at its best was the right one. And why Cleveland? Because this is the home of disc jockey Alan Freed who

Rock and Roll Hall of Fame and Museum, Cleveland, Ohio, 1995.

gave Rock and Roll its name and because the City paid almost half of the $ 92 million cost for the museum.

Once again Pei incorporated geometrics, but as a *New York Times* reviewer wrote, this time the angles have "an Elvis-like swagger." The Rock and Roll Hall of Fame has become a focal point of downtown Cleveland's waterfront redevelopment, very much in keeping with Pei's ideas of urban renewal. Described by Pei as a "tent," the sloping glass triangle of the façade rises five stories. It is enclosed by a tower of concrete and white metal panels. On either side are two wings: a drum shape wrapped by a spiral and perched on a column; and an unusual shape, similar to a stereo speaker, jutting out over the water. The forms are both playful and sculptural, far removed from Pei's John Hancock Tower.

The interior, as in other buildings, opens into a huge, high, light-filled space. Striped cars hang from white metal trusses. Everywhere are balconies, stair-

cases, and escalators to aid in circulation through the exhibit. A disc jockey's booth oversees the entire atrium.

As with the John F. Kennedy Museum, the building is a showcase for the marvelous exhibits. Most of the displays are below ground and separated by style, social and musical history. Some are performance-oriented and some are even interactive! The museum contains additional space for new exhibits and a 200-seat auditorium. Eventually the drum wing will house a dance floor. The Hall of Fame itself is located at the top of the white tower. Here, in a darkened room, names and faces from musical history glow from the walls.

The real action, however, is at the café level, which is a suspended platform where the entire complex is within view. It is this social space that, like the museum itself, pulls people together.

Pei was 70 when he started The Rock and Roll Hall of Fame and Museum. His long and fruitful career has created landmark after landmark. He has been criticized for being too intellectual and modern, but each of his buildings has proved to be perfectly situated, responsive to the environment and completely in touch with its function. In 1986, at the Centennial Celebration of the Statue of Liberty, Pei was one of 12 people awarded the

Medal of Liberty by President Ronald Reagan. This honor is reserved for foreign-born American citizens who have made major contributions to the quality of life in the United States. Pei also received the Japanese Art Association's Premium Imperiale award for lifetime achievement in the arts.

What is next for Pei? When he finished the Rock and Roll Hall of Fame and Museum he said, "I wanted the building to be full of youthful energy. As an old man, I want to find some of that, too!"

SELECTED BIBLIOGRAPHY

GENERAL

Glenn, Patricia Brown. *Under Every Roof: A Kid's Style and Field Guide to the Architecture of American Houses*. New York: Preservation Press/John Wiley & Sons, Inc., 1993, 1996.

Heyer, Paul. *American Architecture: Ideas and Ideologies in the Late Twentieth Century*. New York: Van Nostrand Reinhold, 1993.

Maddex, Diane, editor. *Master Builders: A Guide to Famous American Architects*. New York: Preservation Press/John Wiley & Sons, Inc., 1983.

Le Blanc, Sidney. *20th Century American Architecture*. New York: Whitney Library of Design, Watson-Guptill Publications, 1993.

Poppeliers, John, S. Allen Chambers and Nancy B. Schwartz. *What Style Is It?* New York: Preservation Press/John Wiley & Sons, Inc., 1986.

Scully, Vincent, Jr. *American Architecture and Urbanism*. New York: Henry Holt, 1988.

Scully, Vincent, Jr. *Modern Architecture*. New York: George Brazillier, Inc., 1974.

Thorndike, Joseph J., Jr., editor. *Three Centuries of Notable American Architects*. New York: American Heritage Publishing, Co., 1981.

Tishler, William H., editor. *American Landscape Architecture: Designers and Their Places*. New York: Preservation Press/John Wiley & Sons, Inc., 1983.

Trachtenberg, Marvin and Isabelle Hyman. *Architecture From Prehistory to Post-Modernism*. New York: Harry N. Abrams, Inc., 1986.

THOMAS JEFFERSON

Adams, William Howard, editor. *The Eye of Thomas Jefferson*. Washington, D.C.: National Gallery of Art, 1976.

Frary, I.T. *Thomas Jefferson Architect and Builder*. Richmond: Garrett and Massie, 1936.

Peterson, Merrill D., editor. *Thomas Jefferson: A Reference Biography*. New York: Charles Scribner's Sons, 1986.

FREDERICK LAW OLMSTED

Beveridge, Charles E. and Paul Rocheleau. *Frederick Law Olmsted: Designing the American Landscape*. New York: Rizzoli International, 1995.

Kelly, Bruce; Gail Travis Guillet and Mary Ellen W. Hern. *Art of the Olmsted Landscape*. New York: New York City Landmarks Preservation Commission and The Arts Publisher, Inc., 1981.

Burnham, Louise C. and George W.W. Packard. *Central Park*. New York: Crescent Books, Michael Friedman Publishing Group, Inc., 1993.

Fabos, Julius Gy, Gordon T. Milde and V. Michael Weinmayr. *Frederick Law Olmsted, Sr.: Founder of Landscape Architecture in America*. Boston: University of Massachusetts Press, 1968.

HENRY HOBSON RICHARDSON

Hitchcock, H.R. *The Architecture of H.H. Richardson and His Times*. New York: Museum of Modern Art, 2nd ed. Harnden, Conn.: Archer Books, 1961.

O'Gorman, James F. *H.H. Richardson*. Chicago: The University of Chicago Press, 1987.

O'Gorman, James F. *Three American Architects: Richardson, Sullivan and Wright*. Chicago: The University of Chicago Press, 1991.

LOUIS HENRI SULLIVAN

Condit, C. *The Chicago School of Architecture*. Chicago: The University of Chicago Press, 1964.

De Witt, William, editor. *Louis Sullivan: The Function of Ornament*. New York: W.W. Norton and Company with Chicago Historical Society and the Saint Louis Art Museum, 1986.

Frazier, Nancy. *Louis Sullivan and the Chicago School*. New York: Crescent Books, 1991.

FRANK LLOYD WRIGHT

Pawley, Martin. *Frank Lloyd Wright: Public Buildings*. New York: Simon and Schuster, 1970.

Pfeiffer, Bruce Brooks. *Frank Lloyd Wright Masterworks*. New York: Rizzoli International and the Frank Lloyd Wright Foundation, 1993.

Scully, Vincent. *Frank Lloyd Wright*. New York: Brazillier, 1960.

JULIA MORGAN

Boutelle, Sara Holmes. *Julia Morgan Architect*. New York: Abbeville Press, 1988; revised 1995.

James, Cary. *Julia Morgan: American Women of Achievement*. New York: Chelsea House Publishers, 1990.

Lee, Nancy E. *Hearst Castle: An Interpretive History of W.R. Hearst's San Simeon Estate*. Santa Barbara: Companion Press, 1994.

Longstreth, Richard W. *Julia Morgan Architect*. Berkeley: Berkeley Architectural Heritage Association, 1977.

LUDWIG MIES VAN DER ROHE

Johnson, Philip. *Mies van der Rohe*. 3rd ed. Rev. New York: Museum of Modern Art, 1978.

Pawley, Martin. *Mies van der Rohe*. New York: Simon & Schuster, 1970.

Spaeth, David. *Mies van der Rohe*. New York: Rizzoli International, 1985.

Speyer, A. James. *Mies van der Rohe*. Chicago: The Art Institute of Chicago, 1968.

PAUL R. WILLIAMS

Hudson, Karen E. *Paul R. Williams, Architect: A Legacy of Style*. New York: Rizzoli International, 1993.

Hudson, Karen E. *The Will and the Way: Paul R. Williams, Architect*. New York: Rizzoli International, 1994.

Travis, Jack, editor. *African-American Architects in Current Practice*. New Jersey: Princeton University Press, 1991.

PHILIP JOHNSON

Kazanjian, Dodi. "Philip Johnson's Monsta." *The New Yorker Magazine*. September 11, 1995: 74.

Knight, Carleton, III. *Philip Johnson/John Burgee Architecture 1979-1985*. New York: Rizzoli International, 1985.

Muller, Nory. *Johnson and Burgee Architecture*. New York: Random House, 1979.

Noble, Charles. *Philip Johnson*. New York: Simon & Schuster, 1972.

I.M. PEI

Cannell, Michael. *I.M. Pei: Mandarin of Modernism*. New York: Carol Southern Books, 1995.

"Complicated Shapes, Moving Experiences." *American Institute of Architects Journal*. Mid-May, 1980: 180-189.

"An Interview with I.M. Pei." *Interior Design*. October, 1978: 244-245.

Marlin, William. "Some Reflections on the John Hancock Tower." *Architectural Record*. June, 1977: 117-126.

"Rock and Roll Hall of Fame Museum, Cleveland." *Architectural Record*. September 9, 1994: 32-33.

GLOSSARY

* Note this is not a comprehensive glossary but includes only those architectural terms needing definition in this book.

Antiquarian: An individual who is learned about ancient times, places, and things.

Apprentice: Someone working with a master to learn a trade.

Arcade: A series of arches resting on columns or posts; may have roof.

Arch: A curved masonry opening with the weight supported by piers, columns, or a solid wall. There are several types of arches: semicircular, elliptical, flat, or pointed.

Art Deco: A style of design popularized by the Paris *Exposition Internationale des Artes, Decoratifs et Industrieles Modern* of 1925. Most influential on skyscraper design decorated with angular or zigzag patterns and ornament glorifying the Industrial Age. Also know as the Style Moderne.

Atrium: The central courtyard of a Roman house which is open to the sky and edged by a roof. Today, the atrium is the glass covered central courtyard of a large commercial building.

Bay: The repeated space between vertical elements in a building determined by upright support such as beams or columns.

Belt course: A thin horizontal band across the front or around an entire building. Often of molded wood. Also know as a band or stringcourse.

Board and Batten: Plywood boards or sheets joined by thin wooden strips often used for exterior or interior siding.

Cantilever: A horizontal projecting beam, step, balcony, roof, or any structural element extending beyond the supporting wall or pier. There is no additional external support so the cantilever appears to be self-supporting.

Cartouche: Most often an ornately inscribed and decorated panel with curling edges. Can be a curved form as in a frame.

Cast iron: Iron metal that has been poured into a mold and formed.

Chair rail: A strip of wood or plaster affixed to the wall at chair height and running horizontally around the room to prevent the scraping of a chair back against the wall.

Chancel: The eastern end of a church where the alter is located; reserved for clergy and choir.

Classicism: Style based upon the arts of ancient Rome and Greece.

Clerestory: The upper part of the roof over the aisle in a church pierced by windows; a similar principle is applied in residential architecture too.

Colossal: Having to do with columns that are more than one story tall.

Column: In classical architecture, a tapering, cylindrical post having basically three parts: the base, shaft and capital. Performs a supporting function by carrying an entablature but can stand alone as decorative element.

Commission: An assignment for a work of art or architecture for which the artist or architect is paid.

Corinthian: The most ornate of the three classical orders. It is identified by a slender fluted column and a capital of stylized acanthus leaves.

Cornice: A decorative treatment at the top of a wall or arch; the uppermost part of a classical entablature.

Curtain Wall: A wall that is not load bearing; a screen, between beams or piers of a structural steel building.

Dome: A curved roof, often in a hemispherical shape, covering an area.

Doric: One of the classical orders for a column, very simple and strong in shape.

Draftsman: An individual who creates architectural renderings or drawings for an architect.

Entablature: In classical architecture, the horizontal element supported by columns. It is decorated and scaled differently for each classical order. The entablature has three horizontally arranged major components: architrave, frieze, and cornice.

Environmental Preservationist: An individual with a deep concern for the care and maintenance of the natural environment.

Façade: The front or face of a building.

Floral: Having to do with flowers.

French doors: Also called casement doors. Composed of several panes of glass within a frame of lintel, sill, and stile (an upright piece of the window or door jam usually on the outside). Generally in pairs and opening outward from center.

Gable roof: A triangular-shaped roof with two sloping sides that meet at the vertical ridge and extend to or beyond the cornice.

Gallery or galleria: An extended, covered walkway on the exterior or interior of a building, or between two buildings.

Glazed: A thin coating on pottery; shiny and glossy; glass panes.

Hip Roof or Hipped Roof: Sloping roof that rises upward from all four corners of a building.

I-Beam: Having the pronounced shape of an "I" and made from molded steel.

Ionic: A classical order between Doric and Corinthian characterized by its volutes or spiral scrolls on either side of capital.

École des Beaux-Arts: Located in Paris, a school of fine arts sponsored by the French government. Enjoyed great popularity during the 1800s and 1900s for its architectural studies based on the antique tradition. Its influence can be seen in many buildings in the United States and abroad.

Landscape architect: A trained individual who can determine the most successful and attractive usage for land.

Lintel: The horizontal member between two upright posts.

Masonry: A construction term referring to materials of tile, brick, or stone held together with mortar, plaster, or concrete.

Mural: A painted picture on a wall for decorative purposes; usually narrative in content.

Nave: The long central portion of the church west of the transept or crossing may have aisles on either side.

Ornamentalist: One who is involved in decorating a plain surface through sculpture, painting or some other medium.

Parapet: A low wall around the edge of a roof or balcony.

Piazza: An open public space usually with buildings on all sides.

Piers: A thick vertical support of masonry designed to carry heavy loads—not a column.

Podium: A flat, solid mass of masonry upon which a temple is built; a solid projecting platform for a building.

Porte cochère: A sheltered area for cars (originally for carriages) extending out from the entrance of a building.

Portico: An entry way with a roof supported by columns, which may be open or partially enclosed.

Real estate: Land and buildings.

Reinforced concrete: Concrete that has been strengthened by the addition of steel bars or wire mesh before it is poured.

Sill: The horizontal slab or frame at the bottom of a window.

Spandrels: The panel in a skyscraper below the window sill and on top of the window head below it; it may be decorated.

Stained glass: Pieces of glass colored in a molten state or stained; usually held together by lead. Used to decorate windows.

Stencil: A form with cut-out decorations or letters that enable transfer of that design to a wall or similar surface. The name by which the decoration or letters are called.

Stucco: A finish for walls, usually exterior, made from cement, lime, and sand. Can be sculpted into a decorative ornament.

Terra cotta: Unglazed, fired clay, usually red in color, used for ornamentation and roof and floor tiles.

Transept: That portion of the arch that crosses the nave at right angles forming a cross-shaped plan.

Truss: An architectural framework, composed of primarily triangular pieces, to ensure a strong structural system for a building.

Urban planning: The planning of a town that involves the placement of buildings, circulation of traffic, placement of parks, and so on.

Vernacular: Common to a particular place.

Vestibule: A small room situated between an exterior and interior entrance.

Welded: Uniting two pieces (usually metal) by heating them and letting them bond as they cool.

CREDITS

page 2   Copy of the 1821 Life Portrait of Thomas Jefferson painted by Thomas Sully, 1856. Courtesy of
Monticello/Thomas Jefferson Memorial Foundation, Inc; gift of Mr. and Mrs. Carl W. Smith and Mr. and
Mrs. T. Eugene Worell.

page 10   Courtesy of Thomas Jefferson's Poplar Forest.

page 12   Frederick Law Olmsted, Sr., c. 1895. Courtesy of the National Park Service, Frederick Law Olmsted
National Historic Site.

page 14   Clavert Vaux. Courtesy of the Society for the Preservation of New England Antiquities.

page 22   H. H. Richardson, Architect. Photograph © 1995, The Art Institute of Chicago. All Rights Reserved.

page 30   Louis H. Sullivan, Architect, 1890. Photograph © 1995, The Art Institute of Chicago. All Rights Reserved.

page 32   Dankmar Adler, Architect. Photograph © 1995, The Art Institute of Chicago. All Rights Reserved.

page 40   H & S H273: Portrait of Frank Lloyd Wright, c. 1904-1906, John Lloyd Wright Collection. Courtesy of the
Frank Lloyd Wright Home and Studio Foundation.

page 50   Images of Fallingwater are used with permission from the Western Pennsylvania Conservancy.

page 53   Courtesy of S. C. Johnson Wax.

page 54   Courtesy of S. C. Johnson Wax.

page 58   Julia Morgan, Architect. Special Collections, California Polytechnic State University.

page 66   Hearst San Simeon Historical Monument ™, 1919-1947, San Simeon, California, Julia Morgan
architect. Listed on the National Register of Historic Places, National Historic Landmark and unit of the
California State Park System.

page 70   Mies van der Rohe, Architect. Photograph © 1995, The Art Institute of Chicago. All Rights Reserved.

page 80   Paul R. Williams, Archtect. Paul R. Williams Collection.

page 86   Used with permission of Paul R. Williams Collection.

page 90   Philip Johnson, Architect. © 1989 by Luca Vignelli, photographer, all rights reserved.

page 93   John Burgee, Architect. Courtesy of John Burgee.

page 95   Courtesy of Crystal Cathedral.

page 98   I. M. Pei, Architect. © 1996 Ingbet Grüttner.

page 105 Rock and Roll Hall of Fame and Museum © 1995.

ARCHITECTS AND BUILDINGS IN THIS BOOK

Those building marked "NR" are listed in the National Register of Historic Places which is our nation's way of recognizing buildings of state, local or national interest. Those buildings marked with "NHL" are structures that are on the National Register but are also designated as Historic Landmarks because of their national importance. "NPS" acknowledges those park lands that are significant in the history or composition of our nation's landscapes.

1. THOMAS JEFFERSON, 1743-1826

NR/NHL	1. Monticello, 1768-1809, Charlottesville, Va.
NR/NHL	2. Virginia State Capitol, 1785-1798, Richmond, Va.
NR/NHL District	3. University of Virginia, 1817-1826, Charlottesville, Va. (Jefferson Complex of
NHL Rotunda	Rotunda, Pavillions, and Campus is on World Heritage List).
NR/NHL	4. Poplar Forest, 1806, Bedford County, Va.

2. FREDERICK LAW OLMSTED, 1822-1903

NR/NHL	1. Central Park, 1858-1880, New York, N.Y.
NR/NHL	2. Riverside, Illinois, 1868-1869, Riverside, Il. (Riverside Landscape Architect District).
NR/NHL	3. Niagara Falls, 1869 1885, Niagara, N.Y.

3. HENRY HOBSON RICHARDSON, 1838-1886

NR/NHL	1. Trinity Church, 1872-1877, Boston, Ma.
	2. Marshall Field Wholesale Warehouse, 1883-1887, Chicago, Il. (demolished).
NR/NHL	3. Ames Gate Lodge, 1880-1881, North Easton, Ma. (H.H. Richardson Historic District of North Easton- -NR District and NHL District).
NR/NHL	4. Old Colony Depot, 1881-1884, North Easton, Ma. (H.H. Richardson Historic District. of North Easton—NR District and NHL District.

NR/NHL	5. Thomas Crane Memorial Library, 1880-1882, Quincy, Ma.
NR/NHL	6. Mary Fiske Stoughton House, 1882-1883, Cambridge, Ma.

4. LOUIS HENRI SULLIVAN, 1856-1924

NR/NHL	1. Auditorium Building (Roosevelt University), 1886-1890, Chicago, Il.
NR/NHL	2. Wainwright Building, 1890-1891, St. Louis, Mo.
NR/NHL	3. Schlesinger and Meyer Department. Store (Carson, Pirie, Scott), 1898-1904. Chicago, Il.
NR/NHL	4. National Farmer's Bank (Norwest Bank), 1906-1908, Owatonna, Minn.

5. FRANK LLOYD WRIGHT, 1867-1959

NR/NHL	1. Frank Lloyd Wright's Home 1889 and Studio, 1898, Oak Park, Il.
	2. "Slat Back Chair" from Robie House, 1909, Chicago, Il.
NR/NHL	3. Frederick C. Robie House (University of Chicago), 1909, Chicago, Il.
NR	4. Herbert Jacobs House, 1936, Madison, Wisc.
NR/NHL	5. "Fallingwater", 1936, Mill Run, Pa.
NR/NHL	6. Taliesin West, 1937-1940, Scottsdale, Ariz.
NR/NHL	7. S.C. Johnson and Son Administrative Building, 1936-1939, and Research Tower, 1947-1950, Racine, Wisc.
	8. Solomon R. Guggenheim Museum, 1943-1959, New York, N.Y.

6. JULIA MORGAN, 1872-1957

	1. El Campanile, Mills College, 1904, Oakland, Ca.
	2. Fairmont Hotel, 1906, San Francisco, Ca., reconstruction.
NR/NHL/NPS	3. Hearst's San Simeon, 1919-1947, San Simeon, Ca.
NR/NHL	4. YWCA Conference Center, Asilomar Conference Gates, 1913, Tents, 1913-1917 (demolished) and Merill Hall, 1928 both listed as part of national register district.

7. LUDWIG MIES VAN DER ROHE, 1886-1969

	1. Barcelona Chair, 1926.
	2. MR Chair, 1929.
	3. S.R. Crown Hall, 1950-1958, Illinois Institute of Technology, Chicago, Il.
NR	4. 860-880 Lake Shore Drive Apartments, 1948-51, Chicago, Il.
	5. Seagram Building, 1954-1958, New York, N.Y. (with Philip Johnson).
	6. Farnsworth House, 1945-1950, Plano, Il.

8. PAUL R. WILLIAMS, 1894-1980

1. E. L. Cord Residence, 1931, Beverly Hills, Ca. (demolished).
2. Jay Paley Residence, 1934, Holmby Hills, Ca.
3. Pueblo del Rio Housing Project, 1933-1941, Los Angeles, Ca.
4. Paul R. Williams Residence, 1951, Los Angeles, Ca.
5. Saks Fifth Avenue, 1939, Beverly Hills, Ca. (1949/50 interior only—alterations/additions).
6. Beverly Hills Hotel Polo Lounge, Fountain Coffee Shop and Crescent Wing, 1947-1951, Beverly Hills, Ca.

9. PHILIP JOHNSON, b. 1906-

1. Glass House, 1949, New Canaan, Ct.
2. Pennzoil Place, 1974-1976, Houston, Tx. (Johnson/Burgee).
3. Garden Grove Community Church (Crystal Cathedral), 1976-1980, Garden Grove, Ca. (Johnson/Burgee).
4. AT&T Corporate Headquarters (Sony Building), 1984, New York, N.Y. (Johnson/Burgee).
5. Monsta, 1994-95, New Canaan, Ct.

10. I.M. PEI (Ioeh Ming Pei), b. 1917-

1. Denver Mile High Project, 1956, Denver, Co. (I.M. Pei and Partners *Architects*, I.M. Pei, Design Partner).
2. John Hancock Tower, 1976, Boston, Ma. (I.M. Pei and Partners *Architects*, Henry N. Cobb, Design Partner).
3. National Gallery of Art, East Wing, 1978, Wash., D.C. (I.M. Pei and Partners *Architects*, I.M. Pei, Design Partner).
4. John Fitzgerald Kennedy Library and Museum, 1979, Boston, Ma. (I.M. Pei and Partners *Architects*, I.M. Pei, Design Partner).
5. Rock and Roll Hall of Fame and Museum, 1995, Cleveland, Oh. (Pei Cobb Freed and Partners *Architects*, I.M. Pei, Design Partner).

INDEX

Italicized boldface numbers refer to illustrations on those page numbers.

Adler & Sullivan, 31, 32-36, 42-43
Adler, Dankmar, 32-36, **32,** 43,
    See also Adler & Sullivan
Ames Gate Lodge, 26, **26**
Arizona: Taliesin West, Scottsdale,
    41, 51-52, **52,** 56
Asilomar YWCA Conference Center,
    63-64, **63, 64**
AT&T Corporate Headquarters, 95-96, **96**
Auditorium Building, 33, **33,** 43
Automobile, influence on architecture , 48
Bauhaus School of Design, 74, 91
Beverly Hills Hotel, 88, **88**
Boston Public Library, Copley Square,100
Breuer, Marcel, 73, 91. *See*
    also Furniture
Broadacre City Project, 48
Bryant Building, 36
Burgee, John, 90, 93-96, **93**
Burnham & Root, 31, 42
California:
    Beverly Hills Hotel, Beverly Hills, 88, **88**
    El Campanile, Mills College,
        Oakland, **60,** 61-62
    E.L. Cord Residence, Beverly Hills,
        84-85, **84**
    Garden Grove Community Church,
        Garden Grove, 94-95, **95**
    Jay Paley Residence, Holmby Hills,
        Los Angeles, **85,** 86,
    Paul R. Williams Residence, Los
        Angeles, **86**
    Pueblo de Rio, Los Angeles, 87-88
    Saks Fifth Avenue, Beverly Hills, 87, **87**
    San Simeon, San Simeon, 65-67, **65,**
        66, 68, 69
    Sequoia Big Tree Groves, 18
    Wyntoon on McCloud River, 67-68
    Yosemite Valley, 18
    YWCA Asilomar, 63-64, **63-64**
Casa Grande, San Simeon, 65-67, **65, 66**

Central Park, 14-18, **14,** 15, 17, **16-17**
Chicago fire, 30, **31**
Chicago School of Architecture, 31, 35
Chicago Stock Exchange, 39
Classical Revival, 2. *See also* Jeffersonian
Clérisseau, Charles Louise, 6-7
Colorado: Denver Mile High Center,
    Denver, 100, **100**
Connecticut:
    Glass House, New Canaan, **92,** 92-93
    Monsta, New Canaan, 97, **97**
Denver Mile High Center, 100, **100**
Downing, Andrew Jackson, 14
Dumb waiter table, Monticello, 5, **5**
East Wing of National Gallery of Art
    102, 102-103
École des Beaux Arts, Paris, France,
    22-23, 29, 32, 58-59, 80
860-880 Lake Shore Drive Apartments,
    75, 75-76
El Campanile, Mills College, **60,** 61-62
E.L. Cord Residence, 84-85, **84**
Elevator, 31, **31**
Fairmont Hotel, 62
Fallingwater, 41, **50,** 51
Farnsworth House, 77-78, **78,** 93
Frank Lloyd Wright Foundation, 56
Frank Lloyd Wright Home and Studio,
    42, 43
Frederick C. Robie House, 45-47, **46**
Froebel Blocks, 42
Furness, Frank, 32
Furniture:
    Barcelona Chair, 72-73, **73**
    Mr. Chair, 72-73, **73**
    Slat Back Chair, 45, **45**
    Wassily Chair, 73
Garden Grove Community Church, 94-
    95, **95**
German Pavilion for the International
    Exhibition, 72, **72**
Glass House, **92,** 92-93
Gropius, Walter, 70, 72, 91
Hearst, Phoebe Apperson, 59, 63, 67
Hearst, William Randolph, 59, 65-69
Herbert Jacobs House (Wright), 49-50, **49**

Hitchcock, Henry Russell, 91
Hoban, James, 7
Holabird & Roche, 31, 42
Home Insurance Building, 32, 33
Illinois:
    Auditorium Building, Chicago, 33, 43,
        33
    860-880 Lake Shore Drive Apartments,
        Chicago, **75,** 75-76
    Farnsworth House, Plano, 77-78, **78,**
        93
    Frank Lloyd Wright Home and Studio,
        Oak Park, **42,** 43
    Frederick C. Robie House, Chicago,
        45-47, **46**
    Illinois Institute of Technology, 74-75
    S.R. Crown Hall, **74,** 74-75, 79
    Marshall Field Wholesale Warehouse,
        Chicago, 22, 24-25, **25,** 33
    Riverside, city of, 19-20, **20**
    Schlesinger and Meyer Department
        Store, (Carson, Pirie, Scott), 35-36,
        37
    Transportation Building, Chicago, 36
    World's Columbian Exposition,
        Chicago, 20-21, 36, 61
Illinois Institute of Technology, 74-75, 79
I.M. Pei and Partners, Architects, 100
Industrial Revolution, architecture, 20, 32
International Style, 91, 93
Jay Paley Residence, **85,** 86
Jefferson, Thomas, **2,** 2-11
Jeffersonian, 2. *See also* Classical Revival
Jenney, Major William Le Baron, 32-33, 42
John F. Kennedy Library, 103-104, **104**
John Hancock Tower, 100 102, **101**
Johnson, Philip, **90,** 90-97
Johnson/Burgee, *see* Johnson, Philip *and*
    Burgee, John
Larkin Builidng, 43
Latrobe, Benjamin Henry, 7
Le Corbusier, 72, 91
L'Enfant, Pierre-Charles, 7
Maison Carrèe, Nîmes, France, 6, **6**
Marshall Field Wholesale Warehouse,
    22, 24-25, **25,** 33

Mary Fiske Stoughton House, 28, **29**

Massachusetts Institute of Technology, 31, 32, 99

Massachusetts:

Ames Gate Lodge, North Easton, 26, **26**

John Hancock Tower, Boston, 100-102, **101**

John F. Kennedy Library and Museum, Boston, 103-104, **104**

M.F. Stoughton House, Cambridge, 28, **29**

Old Colony Depot, North Easton, 27, **27**

Thomas Crane Memorial Library, Quincy, 27-28, **28**

Trinity Church, Boston, 23, **24, 101**

Maybeck, Bernard, 59, 61, 67

McKim, Mead & White, 29, 100

Merrill Hall, YWCA, 63-64, **63**

Mies van der Rohe, Ludwig, **70,** 70-79, 91, 92, 93

Mills College, 61-62

Minnesota: National Farmer's Bank, Owatonna, 37-39, **38**

Missouri: Wainwright Building, St. Louis, 33-34, **34**

Monsta, New Canaan, Connecticut, 97, **97**

Monticello, 3-6, **3, 4**

Morgan, Julia, **58,** 58-69, **61**

National Farmer's Bank, 37-39, **38**

National Gallery of Art, West Building, 102-103. *See also* East Wing, National Gallery

New England Transcendentalists, 13

New York:

AT&T Corporate Headquarters, 95-96, **96**

Central Park, 14-18, **14, 15, 16-17**

Four Seasons Restaurant, 76

Niagara Falls Park, Niagara Falls,19, **19**

Seagram Building, 76-77, **77,** 92, 93

Solomon R. Guggenheim Museum, 41, 54-56, **55**

Niagara Falls Park, Niagara Falls, 19, **19**

Ohio: Rock and Roll Hall of Fame and

Museum, Cleveland, 104-107, **105**

Old Colony Depot (Richardson), 27, **27**

Olmsted, Frederick Law, **12,** 12-21, 26, 29

Parks, public, 13-14

Central Park, New York, 14-18, **15, 16-17**

Niagara Falls, New York, 19, **19**

Sequoia Big Tree Groves, California, 18

Yosemite Vally, California, 18

Paul R. Williams Residence, **86**

Pei, I.M., **98,** 98-107

Pennsylvania: Fallingwater, Mill Run, 41, **50,** 51

Pennzoil Place, 94, **94**

Phoebe Apperson Hearst Gymnasium, University of California, Berkeley , 59

Poplar Forest, 11, **10**

Prairie Style, 41, 44-47

President's House (White House), 7

Price Tower, 54

Pueblo del Rio Housing Project, 87-88

Richardson, Henry Hobson, **22, 23,** 22-29, 39, 43

Richardsonian Romanesque, 23-24

Riverside, Illinois, city of, 19-20, **20**

Rock and Roll Hall of Fame and Museum, 104-107, **105**

Saks Fifth Avenue (interior), 87, **87**

S.C. Johnson and Son Administration Building, 52-54, **53, 54**

S.R. Crown Hall, Illinois Institute of Technology, **74,** 74-75, 79

San Simeon, San Simeon, 65-67, **65, 66,** 68, 69

Schlesinger and Meyer Department Store (Carson, Pirie, Scott), 35-36, **37**

Seagram Building, 76-77, **77,** 92, 93

Sequoia Big Tree Groves, 18

Skyscraper, 31, 35, 75

Solomon R. Guggenheim Museum, 41, 54-56, **55**

Spain: Barcelona: German Pavilion for the International Exhibition, 72, **72**

Sullivan, Louis Henri, 22, 29, **30,** 30-39, 43-44, 75

Taliesin, Spring Green, 47-48, 56

Taliesin West, 41, 51-52, **52,** 56

Taliesin Fellowship, 48, 52

Texas: Pennzoil Place, Houston, 94, **94**

Thomas Crane Memorial Library, 27-28, **28**

Transportation Building, 36

Trinity Church, Boston, 23, **24, 101**

Trinity Church, Oak Park, 43

University of Virginia, **8, 9,** 8-11

Usonian House, 49, **49.** *See also* Herbert Jacobs House

Vaux, Calvert, **14,** 14-19

Virginia:

Monticello, Charlottesville, **3, 4,** 3-6

Poplar Forest, Lynchburg, 11, **10**

Rotunda of University of Virginia, Charlottesville, **9,** 9-11

University of Virginia, Charlottesville, 8-11, **8, 9**

Virginia State Capitol, model for, Richmond, 6-7, **6**

Wainwright Building, 33-34, **34**

Washington, D.C.:

design of city, 7, **7**

East Wing, National Gallery of Art, 102-103, **102**

White House, 7

Williams, Paul Revere , **80,** 80-89,

Wisconsin:

Herbert Jacobs House, Madison, 49-50, **49**

S.C. Johnson and Son Administration Building, Racine, 52-54, **53, 54**

Taliesin, Spring Green, 47-48, 56

World's Columbian Exposition, 20-21, 61

Transportation Building, 36

World's Fair, *see* World's Columbian Exposition

Wright, Frank Lloyd, 29, 35, 36, 39, **40,** 40-57

Wyntoon, 67-68

Yosemite Valley Park, 18

Young Women's Christian Association (YWCA), 63-64

YWCA, Asilomar Conference Center, **63, 64,** 63-64